"We live in the era of 'bowling _____ endless cause ____ not only relational but also subs_____ ____ . ____ have experienced community more deeply ____ _____ ____ the cope than in church. It is no_ enough to d__ _____ _ __ ____ grass; we need to recover what is most poten_ _____ faithful, honest, life-changing connection in the community of God. Tom Bennardo has prepared a lavish feast of truth that can change an individual's heart and the momentum of a group to nourish one another with the bread and wine of the coming banquet. Indulge your thirst for intimacy and joy in communion with others, and take in this brilliant book."

Dr. Dan B. Allender, professor of counseling psychology and founding president, The Seattle School of Theology and Psychology

"I'd read this wonderfully instructive book before I opened to the first page. I'd read it because, more than twenty years ago, our family worshiped in the church it is dedicated to. In those transformative years, Tom taught us to risk the honest response to God's Word he details in this book. If you're tired of 'playing church' and ready to experience God's steadfast love for the screwed-up and barely sane, this book is the primer on Christian community you can't do without."

Jen Pollock Michel, author of *A Habit Called Faith* and *In Good Time*

"Tom Bennardo's new book, *Open-Hearted People, Soul-Connected Church*, peels away methodology and programs and speaks to our hearts. It unpacks the Great Commandment and artfully applies it where we live. In the end, all we have will be relationships, and this book ratchets us back to that which is most important—and *most eternal*. Don't miss it."

Dr. Wayne Cordeiro, pastor and author

"In *Open-Hearted People, Soul-Connected Church*, Tom sheds a spotlight on a dimension that the church—especially in North America—seems to be missing. Authentic community is more than something we all long for. It is what we are made for. When we live fully open with Jesus, it doesn't change his relationship with us; it transforms every part of how we relate to him. It frees us to be his body, serving a world that is desperate for that level of relationship. This book is a powerful resource that puts into words what I am praying for all our churches."

Rocky Rocholl, president, Fellowship
of Evangelical Churches

"Tom Bennardo had me when explaining the three levels of honesty. I never knew there was a deeper level than trust and vulnerability, but sure enough 'level 3 honesty' is exactly what we've been missing in our churches. The 'last 10 percent' of our true thoughts and feelings is the type of honesty we need with trusted others, and it is the type King David had with God in Psalm 139:23, when he said, 'Search me, God, and know my heart.'"

Dr. Jay Forseth, former General Superintendent,
The Evangelical Church

"Words like *authenticity* and *vulnerability* can be deeply beneficial, but in today's culture they can also quickly devolve into pithy buzzwords that hold little meaning. However, Tom's thoughtful, practical, and hopeful perspective breathes life back into these important words. Reading this book will require you to press into wisdom, courage, and patience, but here's the good news: it's completely worth the effort. If you long to live your life with authenticity and vulnerability—and not merely talk about it—this book will help you do just that."

J. R. Briggs, author of *The Sacred Overlap* and
Fail and founder, Kairos Partnerships

"Just when you thought you had read enough on friendships, community, and the church, Tom Bennardo's latest offering ups the ante by providing a rich, biblical evaluation of one of the keys to relationships: honest vulnerability. Readers will be challenged and galvanized for a life of community in their local church. I highly recommend."

Jonathan D. Holmes, executive director,
Fieldstone Counseling

"Great relationships come with great risk and even greater reward. Tom Bennardo brilliantly unpacks God's invitation to experience great relationships in *Open-Hearted People, Soul-Connected Church*. Rather than promoting the 'try harder' or 'do better' approach, Tom invites us to first sit with our Savior and experience his amazing grace in full view of our brokenness and to then let his healing grace flow through us into the lives of others. If the idea of opening your true self to others invokes apprehension or even fear, this book will help you. The risk is well worth the reward."

Robert Watson, pastor and author of *Simply Following Jesus*

"Open-Hearted People, Soul-Connected Church" by Tom Bennardo is an important and super helpful book. Read it if you want to understand the deeper levels of our human experience and of Christian fellowship. Bennardo shows us the fellowship God intends for us that too few Christians in our churches experience. This is a great book for everyone but especially for church leaders who need guidance on how to get to deeper levels of heart transparency."

Dr. Bobby Harrington, pastor, author, and CEO,
Discipleship.org and Renew.org

"Tom Bennardo invites, challenges, and guides the reader into a warm, soul-searching quest to discover and revel in relational authenticity with Jesus and others. His illustrations and descriptions are delightfully colorful as they beckon the reader to venture from the safety of the shallows into deeper waters of authenticity. This book offers a pathway from culturally instilled pretense to liberation of the soul and the freedom to be the real you that Christ desires."

Randall A. Bach, ambassador to denominations,
National Association of Evangelicals

"If you accept Tom Bennardo's bold invitation to live in the light as Christ is in the light, the experience itself will profoundly transform the dark places of your life. Living in the light only happens in authentic, beyond-the-mask relationships. So read *Open-Hearted People, Soul-Connected Church* with a friend or two, and walk into the stunning light of a hundred different freedoms you could not have imagined the Trinity had waiting for you."

Dr. Bruce McNicol, president emeritus, Trueface, coauthor
of *The Cure*, *Bo's Cafe*, and *The Ascent of a Leader*

"In recent years, much has been written about the growing awareness of a cultural hunger for authenticity and real community. With this book, Tom Bennardo goes beyond describing the need and honestly addresses how we as individuals and faith communities can live out our God-inspired call to abundant living. This volume is a must-read for those who are honestly seeking a biblical foundation and practical next steps to open their hearts to genuine Christian community."

Dr. Carl P. Greene, executive director, Seventh Day Baptist General Conference of USA and Canada; adjunct instructor, Trinity Evangelical Divinity School

"Being able to lead from the heart is of utmost importance for those leading ministries today. Possessing a force of personality, organizing efficient structures, and setting up reliable systems all have a place in good leadership, but apart from the Holy Spirit, they are not enough to be of true benefit to those we lead. Tom gets that and boldly envisions a leader who authentically abides with Jesus and genuinely connects with people. *Open-Hearted People* is both a testament for leaders who love Jesus and a textbook for how the Holy Spirit forms the leader."

Todd Fetters, bishop, Church of the United Brethren in Christ

"When I began reading *Open-Hearted People, Soul-Connected Church*, I was confident that I would be excited to share it as a very helpful resource and tool for the spiritual journeys of those whom I strive to come alongside and encourage. Not only did it greatly exceed this hope but I also found Tom's practical, biblical insights to be stimulating, refreshing, and concretely helpful in my own walk with our Savior. Tom leaves me even more eager for deeper spiritual growth as he gently urges us to open our hearts to experience and receive what Christ amazingly offers to each of us."

Steve Adriansen, director, Behind the Scenes Ministries

"This book provides practical steps and ideas for a church to become an authentic community where people share a common faith in the Lord and a common trust in each other. The author delves into the benefits of soul-level connectivity and helps people understand the nature of true biblical koinonia. Tom Bennardo makes it clear that it's worth the risk to venture into this level of faithful trust with other believers."

Ron Hamilton, conference minister, Conservative Congregational Christian Conference

Open-Hearted People

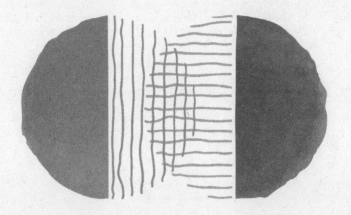

Soul-Connected Church

How Courageous Authenticity Can Transform Your Relationships, Your Community, and Your Life

TOM BENNARDO

BakerBooks

a division of Baker Publishing Group
Grand Rapids, Michigan

Published by Baker Books
a division of Baker Publishing Group
Grand Rapids, Michigan
BakerBooks.com

Printed in the United States of America

Library of Congress Cataloging-in-Publication Data
Names: Bennardo, Tom, author.
Title: Open-hearted people, soul-connected church : how courageous authenticity can transform your relationships, your community, and your life / Tom Bennardo.
Description: Grand Rapids, Michigan : Baker Books, a division of Baker Publishing Group, [2025]
Identifiers: LCCN 2024012132 | ISBN 9781540904607 (paper) | ISBN 9781540904751 (casebound) | ISBN 9781493449125 (ebook)
Subjects: LCSH: Communities—Religious aspects—Christianity.
Classification: LCC BV4517.5 .B45 2025 | DDC 250—dc23/eng/20240711
LC record available at https://lccn.loc.gov/2024012132

Some names and details have been changed to protect the privacy of the individuals involved.

Cover design by Derek Thornton, Notch Design

Baker Publishing Group publications use paper produced from sustainable forestry practices and postconsumer waste whenever possible.

25   26   27   28   29   30   31   7   6   5   4   3   2   1

To Life Community Church of Hilliard,
who embraced Christ's call to be an
open-hearted, soul-connected people,
and continue to live it out.

Contents

Introduction

The vision was compelling. Or so we thought.

We were planting a new church in Columbus, Ohio, painting vivid mental pictures of a place where people could be honest, raw, and real. An authentic community where they would be accepted as they were and could come as they are. Where they'd find support for the burdens they carry and a genuine connection with the God who knows them completely and loves them relentlessly, flaws and all.

Almost without exception, people responded with earnest enthusiasm:

"That's exactly what I've been looking for."
"Now that's a church I would attend."
"I've always wished there could be a place like that."
"Sign me up right now."

And then . . . something happened. When we gathered and invited them to participate in that kind of environment, other almost-universal responses would kick in. Hesitation.

Awkwardness. Resistance. People got weird. They'd grow defensive and uncomfortable. They'd shift and squirm and change the subject, give vague answers, and distance themselves. Many would find reasons not to return. The same eager respondents who said they desperately desired a place to truly open their hearts would keep them tightly shut, then simply drift away.

Something curious occurs when we consider living from a fully opened soul. There's an initial rush—an undeniable sense of its rightness, a craving for its promised freedom. But almost as quickly an internal aversion rises to oppose it. An intense guardedness. A reticence to expose the truest parts of ourselves. More often than not, the latter impulse trumps the former.

There's a reason.

From the time we are kids, we're given explicit instructions for keeping safe in a dangerous world:

"Don't talk to strangers."
"Never get in the car with someone you don't know."
"Don't tell people where you live."

We get a little older and the warnings expand to our possessions:

"Don't share your password."
"Never give out your social security number."
"Don't reply to emails from Nigerian princes."

Eventually the self-protection rules extend to our relationships:

"Don't admit weakness."
"Never let anyone see you cry."
"Trust no one."

So we learn to construct elaborate defense systems to prevent others from seeing our innermost selves, much less from gaining access to them. We elude and evade. We create diversions and misdirection. Magicians master "sleight of hand" to conceal their tricks; we develop "sleight of heart" to keep our true condition at bay. We live among others but maintain a safe distance from them, our souls ensconced behind an invisible, protective wall.

Enter the social media age and its addictive invitation to create artificial versions of ourselves through the wonder of technology. With a keystroke, we can produce digitally altered personas and staged illusions of our lifestyles. Personal interactions are filtered through text messages that allow time for calculated responses. Post-pandemic-era meetings have been reduced to two-dimensional video calls where no one can smell our breath or read our nonverbals or even see if we're wearing pants. At a time when the world most desperately needs—and inwardly craves—genuine connection, we've never had more pressure, or slicker tools, to keep it at bay. Everyone's partially hidden. Carefully guarded. "Safer."

And it's sucking the life out of us.

Our hearts are designed for something radically different: a life-giving connectedness born of deeply formed intimacy, a soul-saturated honesty that stands in striking contrast to the deadened superficiality we see almost everywhere we go.

It's a universal longing. "We all are born into the world looking for someone looking for us," psychiatrist and author Curt Thompson writes in *The Soul of Shame*. "And . . . we remain in this mode of searching for the rest of our lives."[a] We feel it instinctively. We can see it described in Scripture. But the world and our fleshly nature conspire to veer us off its path, convincing us the risks outweigh the rewards. As a result we find ourselves in a state of personal detachment, soul-parched in a relational desert, pretending we're satisfied while we're dying of thirst.

The church might be expected to insert itself here and offer an oasis in that desert, a safe haven where transparency is celebrated and welcomed. But too often we discover its gatherings to be every bit as hostile to self-exposure as the rest of the world. Religious communities are notorious for generating their own brand of pressure to adopt a prescribed image, one that conforms to long-established expectations: behavioral mores, political affiliations, theological positions. Attendees feel compelled to construct spiritual avatars to navigate these settings, deciding their secrets are best left hidden. Authenticity and vulnerability are given lip service, but the church can ultimately become just another place where one set of heart-masking tools is exchanged for another.

There's something else. I work extensively with pastors and Christian leaders. I'm one myself. Many convey a passion to form genuine, open-hearted community where people can drop their guard, share their true selves, and offer each other acceptance, safety, and grace. But the more closely I've worked with spiritual leaders, the more I've discovered that many of the same shepherds who urge full transparency in others don't actually live it themselves. They teach it and champion it, but the image they present to those they lead is itself veiled in self-protection and seldom discloses their true condition. Consequently they never quite produce the environment they say they desire . . . because they're writing travel brochures for places they've never been.

We're longing for something but don't know how to find it. We know we're built for it; we're just unable to enact it. Or unwilling.

It's time to embrace what we were created for. To decide we're weary of the pretense and guardedness. To empower our hearts to do what they were always meant to do.

God intends our souls to live unencumbered by fear and self-protection, opened wide to encounter our world and God himself in healthy, vibrant ways. It's the essence of what Jesus called "life"[b]—maximized human aliveness. When our hearts live in absolute security, gentle openness, and genuine freedom, *zoé* reaches its optimal level. We move closer to experiencing in real time Christ's words, "I have come that they may have life [*zoé*], and have it to the full."[1]

This is a book about your heart—your honest, truest self. How to engage it at what we'll call Level 3 honesty; how to expose it to a recurring Jesus touch that injects it with a liberating, empowering humility; and how to remove the obstructions standing in the way of its most genuine expression to unlock a fundamentally better way to approach its world.

———

A couple things before we start: You're not immediately going to like some of this. Parts of what you'll read may feel unnatural and uncomfortable at first. You'll be invited to exercise some personal and relational muscles you may not have previously developed. That's always painful. The more you work them, the stronger they'll become, but expect some discomfort along the way.

1. John 10:10.

You may also find yourself raising some objections to the level of risk involved in living with the soul-honest transparency we'll explore. You may have questions about how easily an unguarded heart can be abused and how wide a path of vulnerability should be offered. There's definitely wisdom needed to live out the kind of authenticity we'll see laid out in Scripture. We'll address that. Our hesitations won't make the Bible's principles any less true, but they'll test how willing we are to live them out.

At the end of the day, this journey will bring us to one central, pivotal question: Can you open your heart? Or better, will you? How you ultimately answer that question will go a long way toward determining the degree to which you'll experience the profound personal vibrancy and life-changing community God makes available to you.

And if the answer is yes, here's as close to a promise as I can offer, drawn from decades of equipping leaders and individuals to pursue and cultivate a life lived in soul-revealing honesty: Once you see it, you can't unsee it. Once you taste it, you'll find it impossible to do without it. Once you know it, you'll never be satisfied with less. You'll be gloriously ruined.

Because it's the life God intended when he bestowed us with the wonder of a soul. It's what you were made for. A courageously authentic, relentlessly honest, genuinely healthy way of living lies ahead.

You're invited.

1

Three Levels of Honesty

People like to say their life is an open book. What you see is what you get. They have nothing to hide.

Don't believe it.

There's a "you" that you present to your world. This "you" reads the room, measures your words, and reveals carefully selected portions of yourself deemed appropriate to your audience. Others around you return the favor, exchanging pleasantries and ensuring a level of shared geniality. It's an unwritten social contract. And it's virtually universal.

Psychologists commonly illustrate this tendency by pointing to the natural phenomenon observed in icebergs. Before their reputation was sullied by disaster films and their cheesy love ballads, icebergs stood as one of nature's great wonders. Suspended magically in the sea, they exhibit what's known as Archimedes's principle of buoyancy, which results in only 11 percent of an iceberg's mass appearing visibly above the ocean's surface. The remaining 89 percent resides unseen

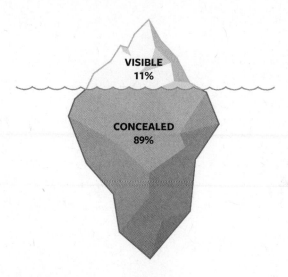

beneath the waterline, invisible to the eye but undefeated in head-to-head battle with ocean liners.

Humans reflect a very similar pattern in the way we present ourselves to our world. We reveal only a fraction of our total selves to public view, with the great majority of our true thoughts, emotions, and histories hidden beneath the surface. We're thus said to function on two levels: the visible, that which is seen above the waterline, and the concealed, that which remains unexposed beneath it.

This isn't news to most of us. We see it, live it, and generally accept it as an accurate picture of human interaction. But look a little closer and we'll see there's more to it—and to us—than the iceberg analogy portrays.

Level 1

What's found above the waterline—what we can call Level 1—represents the externals of our lives. These are the visible, observable elements we routinely present to our world. Here

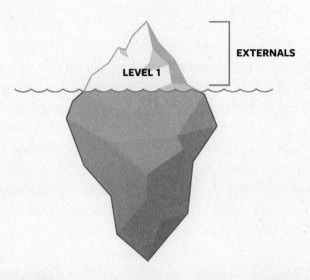

we reveal the pertinent facts about ourselves: our history and qualities, likes and dislikes, skills and passions, involvements and associations.

At Level 1, we'll gladly offer some further details and opinions if people are interested. And sometimes even if they're not. We lean over the backyard fence and share all about our gluten-free diets, our children's achievements, and that time we helped our high school team win the championship.[a] We express our views on everything from what the Fed should do with interest rates, to where to find the best sushi, to which movie most contributed to ruining the *Star Wars* franchise. We compliment the new library they're building and complain about the weather, gas prices, and in-laws.

People we interact with at Level 1 are essentially acquaintances. What they learn of us are the particulars most anyone with whom we've spent time could say they've observed. Myriad details of our lives may be revealed, but they're mostly public knowledge and trivia, the stuff of a Wikipedia page.

Still, at Level 1 we can unite around common causes and share significant bonding moments. I once stood with a capacity crowd at Ohio Stadium and watched as the Ohio State Buckeyes mounted an impossible comeback, tying the game on the last play of regulation and then winning in double overtime. Suddenly a hundred thousand fans were jumping and high-fiving, embracing each other and celebrating like we'd just witnessed the liberation of Paris. The bruising guy next to me—who I'd never seen before in my life—gave me the biggest bear hug I've ever received. He literally kissed the top of my head. For all I knew, he could have been a mass murderer or carrying some communicable disease. In that moment it didn't matter. We were forever bonded by a shared, above-the-waterline experience. And I wasn't even a Buckeyes fan.

You probably don't have trouble thinking of people with whom you relate at Level 1, because it's practically everyone you encounter. In fact, much of what passes for Christian fellowship actually occurs at this level.[b] We stand around holding coffee cups in rooms dubbed "fellowship halls," chatting about family vacations and home improvement projects, ministry programs and our loved one's health. We provide correct answers in group Bible studies and sing worship songs alongside the same people every week, bringing the occasional casserole to potlucks and smiling when our "God is good, all the time" declaration is met with an "All the time, God is good" reply.

Everything just described operates above the waterline, without exposing our private thoughts or offering any glimpse into what's happening below the surface. Because all of this can be done with at least a measure of integrity, what we reveal here can rightly be called Level 1 honesty. It's technically factual and objectively true. But it's an honesty

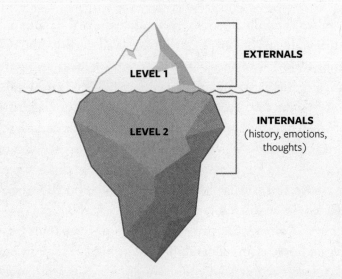

devoid of full authenticity. It's true but not substantive, accurate but not complete. Relational guardrails keep the traffic of our lives on the main road, seldom veering off into the ditches of our weaknesses, past pain, or hidden passions.

Level 2

Below the waterline—what can be called Level 2—a more complete picture of our character and history resides. These are the internals we generally keep hidden: our more controversial thoughts and feelings, the untold details of our life-shaping events, the mistakes we've made and the regrets we carry.

At times, what lies below the waterline is forced to the surface by crisis or betrayal. But more often we only choose to venture into Level 2 when we decide enough trust has been earned to move a relationship from acquaintance to companion, or even friend. To do so we determine it's time to play the uncut version of our life's movie.

So we carefully and incrementally expose the more un-comfortable elements of our history and personality: the eating disorder we once battled, the abusive relationship we suffered, the messy divorce we endured. There's the bank-ruptcy filing, the depression diagnosis, the miscarriage. It's classified information, reserved exclusively for those with se-curity clearance—which only a select few are granted. But to those who are, we're essentially saying, "Okay, this is where I've been, this is what I've done, and this is how I've been affected. Now you know the whole story."

Level 2 introduces two new players to the game: trust and its first cousin vulnerability. We recognize that deeper relationship requires fuller disclosure, so we share our more painful memories, our broken dreams, our severe disappoint-ments. We roll back our sleeves and show our scars.

You can probably name just about everyone you've in-vited into this circle of trust. It's likely not a large number, and you undoubtedly count them among your most trusted confidants and closest friends.

For Christians, Level 2 is where most typical "sharing and caring" happens. We reveal more of ourselves to those we trust will respond with grace and understanding, feeling positive about establishing a safe community where others know the less-than-idyllic aspects of our lives and still care enough to stick with us.

And yet, Level 2 honesty still retains a carefully cultivated element of self-protection. What we expose may be accurate and honest, but its revelations are generally concentrated on the past. The issues have for all intents and purposes been dealt with, their statute of limitations expired. And in most of the stories we recount, we cast ourselves as victim rather than villain because, well, that's honestly how we remember it.

Level 2 contains a subconscious curb that prevents us from rolling into positions of deep, uncomfortable risk. There's more to the story, more to the motives, more to the effects. Something is still held back.

And this is where the iceberg metaphor breaks down. It distinguishes two levels: externals and internals. But even after we engage them we're left perplexed, wondering why we still feel disconnected. Relationally incomplete. Emotionally unsatisfied. Not completely free. We sense there's something beyond what's contained in those two realms.

That's because there's a third level.

Level 3

Beneath (or, perhaps more accurately, within) the iceberg lies another level of our personhood—a place most seldom go

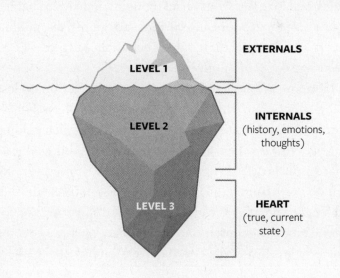

and some don't even know exists. It's the realm of our most authentic self, where the unqualified truth of both who and how we are *at this very moment* resides.

God has a name for this place. He calls it your heart.

Before you roll your eyes at that word for its overuse in everything from pop songs to Hallmark cards, pause for a moment and consider the reality behind the clichés. Modern culture talks about the heart in a thousand frothy phrases: "I love you with all my heart." "Valentine, give me your heart." "I say this from the bottom of my heart." But its roots are found in an extraordinary component of human design.

Your heart is a very real thing.

The Old Testament labels it your *nephesh*—the image-bearing element God breathed into our first father, Adam, that made him a "living soul."[c] It encases not only your beliefs, emotions, and volition but also the utter truth of your current condition: your inmost motives and attitudes; your in-this-moment degree of God-awareness; your weaknesses, aches, and longings; your secret thoughts and hidden habits; your dreams and hopes, insecurities and doubts, disappointments and heartaches. It's deep below the surface—Level 3—where your truest self resides.

Humans are not inclined to acknowledge, much less bring attention to, this inmost place. But it's precisely here that God concentrates nearly his entire focus when guiding our lives toward their healthiest potential. "Above all else, guard your heart," Proverbs 4:23 declares, "for everything you do flows from it." The Bible so consistently establishes the opened heart as the epicenter of God's instructions for interacting with himself and others that, when we become aware of it, it can trigger a Baader-Meinhof effect where you notice something for the first time, then suddenly start seeing it everywhere:

- Speak the truth *from the heart*.[1]
- Draw near to God *with your heart*.[2]
- Love each other deeply *from the heart*.[3]
- Forgive your brother or sister *from your heart*.[4]
- Sing and make music *in your heart* to the Lord.[5]
- Love the Lord *with all your heart*.[6]
- Serve *from your heart*.[7]
- Praise the Lord *with your heart*.[8]
- Do the will of God *from your heart*.[9]
- Open wide *your hearts*.[10]

We're designed by a heart-focused God to live from a heart-honest place. And if our heart represents our truest self, that means doing something our fallen nature is not prone to do: volunteering an unfiltered view of not only our attractive and purified parts but also our shadow side. The current internal battles and temptations we're facing. The recent choices and behaviors we've indulged. The continuing effects past abuses are having on us. The unfinished business we're carrying. It's all part of our true self, our heart.

Level 3 honesty, then, exposes how we're *really* doing, including what is sometimes called the "last 10 percent" of our true thoughts, feelings, and behaviors. It's the current state of our soul—unsanitized and untempered, unmasked and undiluted.

1. Psalm 15:2.   2. Hebrews 10:22.   3. 1 Peter 1:22.   4. Matthew 18:35.
5. Ephesians 5:19.   6. Deuteronomy 6:5.   7. Deuteronomy 10:12.
8. Psalms 9:1; 86:12; 111:1; 138:1.   9. Ephesians 6:6.   10. 2 Corinthians 6:13.

It follows that there's a fundamental difference between Level 3 honesty and the candor we might express at Levels 1 or 2. Think of it this way: if I told you about a dark time in my past when I considered taking my own life, you may feel some surprise and express some sympathy. It would inform your understanding of how my journey has shaped me. That's Level 2 honesty. But if I told you I'm wrestling with thoughts of self-harm right now—today—my words would almost certainly produce a different effect. You'd become significantly more aware of who I really am in the here and now. You'd see into my heart. And you would probably feel a tug to enjoin our hearts in a deeper, more substantive way. That is Level 3 honesty.

Right about now is where you may be tempted to stop reading. Let's face it, nobody feels motivated to be that exposed naturally. "Yeah, buts" and objections jump up to argue that such a level of honesty and vulnerability feels irresponsible, unnecessary, even foolish.

If that's what you noticed bubbling up as you read the descriptions in the previous paragraphs, it's a good indicator you're grasping what God is talking about when he invites us to live from an unguarded heart. Doing something our soul craves but our flesh resists requires a deliberate act of the will and an unnatural measure of courage. It doesn't happen casually or easily. It's why the Bible describes this part of ourselves, the "purposes" of our hearts, as "deep waters" that must be drawn out if they're going to be engaged.[11]

Allow me to pause here and ask an honest question: Is there a place where this level of interaction happens in your

11. Proverbs 20:5.

current relationships? Who do you allow to see this deeply within you? I'm not asking if you experience it everywhere, with everyone. I'm asking if it happens anywhere, with anyone.

If not, it's understandable. Choosing to live with Level 3 honesty carries profound ramifications. It makes your heart visible, touchable—and therefore vulnerable. Your inmost self is now subject to being influenced. Challenged. Criticized. Even wounded or shamed. But as we'll see, when enacted in pure and healthy ways, Level 3 honesty also positions your heart to be meaningfully connected. Accepted. Cared for. Strengthened. Healed. It creates a bond we can't experience otherwise, both with God and with those who serve as instruments of his grace.

The personal, spiritual health that emerges from living at Level 3 honesty is where we're headed with the rest of this book. As we move toward it, we'll do so assuming two things to be true of you:

1. You desire the joy, fullness, and freedom that openhearted honesty can produce within you.
2. You're facing formidable resistance to it.

Tackling that resistance is what we'll explore next.

2

Why We Keep
Our Hearts Hidden

My friend Todd's true-story conversation at the airport check-in counter:

Todd: "Hi. We're checking these two bags."

Airline agent: "Anything fragile, flammable, combustible, or explosive?"

Todd, turning to his wife: "Honey, where did we pack those explosives?"

Airline agent:

Suddenly present armed security guards: "Sir, please step away from the bags and come with us."

Todd's wife: *facepalm*

Todd was detained two hours, and his name put on a watch list.

Anyone with half a brain, which apparently doesn't include Todd, knows there's a list of words you simply don't say at the airport: *bomb, gun, explode, terrorist, hijack.* (Be careful calling out a greeting when you see your buddy Jack across the terminal.) A TSA agent once warned me never to even mention anything about my shoes. Certain statements trigger automatic lockdowns.

Something similar can happen with our souls. We hear the invitation to move toward the freedom found living at Level 3—to open our hearts wide and embrace it—and immediately something within us issues an imminent threat alert and orders us to shut it back down.

Why? Because we've learned from experience. The list is long of unwanted outcomes that all too often accompany self-exposure, and you've likely experienced more than one of them.

Rejection and condemnation. Revealing the genuine state of our souls often results in rebuke, criticism, and judgment. We've seen the weak criticized and the failed ostracized. Sadly, Christians are sometimes among the worst culprits of this, enacting a scorched-earth policy that eviscerates those who stumble and withdraws from those who expose flaws. We shoot our wounded and eat our young.[1]

Betrayal and abuse. Our confidential words, opinions, and histories have been used against us and, at times, wielded as weapons to wound us. When my middle school best friend, Toby, and I were invited to a sleepover at a classmate's house, I told him I was nervous to go and confided my most private secret: I was still prone to wet the bed—something no twelve-year-old boy would ever want revealed to anyone, especially

1. Galatians 5:15.

his peers. Toby and I went together, and at breakfast time he brought it up as a joke in front of the entire group. In that moment three things happened simultaneously: he got a big laugh, I felt utterly emasculated, and a steel door slammed shut inside my heart. It would be years before I would choose to divulge another secret.

No cut pierces so deep as the one inflicted by someone to whom we entrusted the knife. David wrote: "If an enemy were insulting me, I could endure it; if a foe were rising against me, I could hide. But it is you, a man like myself, my companion, my close friend, with whom I once enjoyed sweet fellowship at the house of God, as we walked about among the worshipers."[2] All it takes is one major betrayal—when someone uses something we disclosed in a vulnerable moment to undermine us or advance their own agenda—to convince us we must never, ever give anyone the power to hurt us like that again.

Repercussion and loss. A pastor friend made the decision to admit he sometimes struggles with doubts about what he believes and about the exclusivity of Christianity's truth claims. He acknowledged it in an honest moment with his elder team, as part of their shared resolve to create a safe place where they could be "real" with each other. Afterward, two of the elders reported what they heard to others in the church body. Within days, a congregational meeting was called, the pastor's disclosure was confirmed, and the church's membership forced his resignation. "We can't have someone with those kinds of weaknesses leading us," they said. My friend lost his position, his church family, and his livelihood.

2. Psalm 55:12–14.

When we reveal our true opinions, share our untold histories, and express the struggles we currently face, friendships can be lost. Opportunities can be withdrawn. Relationships can permanently rupture. "If that got back to my boss, I would be fired," we portend. "If my spouse found out about that, my marriage would be over." And we may be right.

Disappointment and unhelpful response. We've all experienced it. In the midst of a suffering season, we express our anguish, and someone responds in a way intended to encourage or help, but that only deepens the pain:

"I know exactly how you feel."

"God will work it all out for good."

"It just wasn't meant to be."

"Don't worry."

"Everything's going to be okay."

"It could be worse."

My wife and I experienced what the medical field calls "secondary infertility" after the birth of our first child. For years we attempted to conceive again without success, enduring an endless string of medical tests and procedures. Every month we would hope, pray, and wait, and every month nature would deliver what felt like another mini death.

We shared our private heartache with a friend who, in an attempt to comfort us, responded, "Well, at least you already have one child."

Those words weren't helpful; they were soul-crushing. They implied we didn't have a legitimate reason to grieve, then piled shame on top of our sadness for not being mature enough to find contentment in what God had previously given us.

If honest admissions of weakness are met with empty platitudes, hollow promises, or even worse, indifference, we're no better off than if we had kept the hurt to ourselves.

Unwanted obligation. When we acknowledge something is wrong, we position ourselves to be pressured into taking responsibility to remedy it. Then we feel constrained to seek help and enact painful processes or to alter our choices and lifestyle. Ignorance isn't always bliss, but it's usually less demanding than the obligation brought on by awareness. It's simply easier to ignore the discolored mole, hope the wet spot on the ceiling dries on its own, and avoid asking the mechanic why the check engine light is on.

Little perceived value. A simple cost-benefit analysis reveals that the return on an open-hearted approach to our world seldom matches the investment. People don't typically know what to do with the truth. They mishandle it, react poorly to it, and stumble through awkward attempts to solve problems they have no capacity to solve. It may sound noble to say our lives are an open book, but it doesn't seem to do us much good to let anyone read its pages.

The Enemy Within

You've witnessed these consequences, and others like them, firsthand. Specific faces and situations probably come to mind as you read them. Together they conspire to push the door to your heart closed and keep it closed.

But the strongest pressure of all is the one that comes from within your heart itself. It's the awareness of just how foul an evil lurks within it and how devastating the shame would be if you let it show. Though we'd like to believe pop culture's sentimental insistence that the human heart is basically good, at our core we're uncomfortably aware of the ugly truth. The sin disease Adam and Eve contracted at the fall of humankind corrupted their nature on a cellular level, mutating until the heart became fundamentally dark. Scripture calls it "deceitful above all things and beyond cure."[3] And it's hereditary.

We may not readily admit it, but we instinctively know it. We're all too aware of the appalling images, thoughts, and feelings our hearts are capable of devising: lusts, judgments, intense selfishness, ill wishes directed toward others. As a kid in Brooklyn, I stood on the crowded subway platform and felt the sudden, intense urge to push the stranger in front of me onto the tracks as the train approached. It horrified me. I feared I must be some kind of closet psychopath . . . until later, when I learned how commonly people report having the same twisted impulse. But that was only one of ten thousand deviant inclinations my heart conceived in my youth. No one planted them in me; they germinated naturally within my own soul.

My adult self has produced thoughts and emotions every bit as degenerate. I don't walk around trumpeting them (and thankfully don't act on them usually), but my heart continues to be the silent spawning ground of unthinkable wickedness.

So is yours. And you're undoubtedly as relieved as I am that no one can read our minds, that there's no video screen where our inmost thoughts can be projected for the world to see.[4] We shudder to think what would happen if there were. Jesus summarized the condition of every breathing person when

3. Jeremiah 17:9.   4. At least not yet—Luke 12:2–3.

he said, "For out of the heart come evil thoughts—murder, adultery, sexual immorality, theft, false testimony, slander."[5]

And then there's this: Adam and Eve's sin not only ruptured their innocence and birthed self-awareness of their inadequacy (their "nakedness"), it also introduced a powerful new force to their souls—fear. The prospect of pain and loss leapt into their psyche. They felt the cold blade of shame against their throats. Vulnerability to disgrace and indignity threatened their security and introduced the very real possibility of judgment and condemnation.

So they did what their now-corrupted nature compelled them to do. They hid. Desperate to avoid exposure, they fashioned coverings and crouched in the foliage to elude their Maker's view. When God called Adam out to reveal himself, he replied, "I heard you in the garden, and I was afraid because I was naked; so I hid."[6]

We've been hiding ever since.

We do so because our heart carry the same disease. They naturally retract to conceal our inadequacies. Our depraved condition recoils to remain hidden, using our bodies as human shields to protect our truest selves from the threat of exposure. Fear slams our souls shut.

For all these reasons it's easy to decide that exposing our hearts simply isn't worth it. We instead send both verbal and nonverbal messages to those around us: "Move along. Nothing to see here." We construct veneers to give the illusion that our lives are open when they're not, using diversionary tactics and unchallengeable phrases, such as:

"I'm a private person."
"It's personal."

5. Matthew 15:19.   6. Genesis 3:10.

"Some things are best kept to oneself."

"It's really nobody's business."

"That's between God and me."

"No need to air dirty laundry."

"What's past is past."

"Let's not go there."

Or we simply avoid heart-exposing environments and relationships altogether, content to maintain a safe personal distance.

The High Price of Concealment

Choosing to live from an unhidden heart most certainly comes with a price—one most consider not worth paying. But a closed-off soul exacts an even greater toll, with some deep-seated, far-reaching effects.

It isolates us. As we will see, the soul is built for clear-channeled connection with others, drawing strength from fellow carriers of the same God-image we bear. When the channel is closed, we find ourselves detached, disconnected in any substantive way from the care and support found in heart-level relationships. Twelve percent of Americans indicate they don't have a single close friend (up from three percent in 1990), and almost half have three or fewer.[a] Personal loneliness is now considered an epidemic in our society.[b]

And it's a silent killer. "I saw something meaningless under the sun," the writer of Ecclesiastes laments. "There was a man all alone."[7] He then adds this sobering commentary: "If either of them falls down, one can help the other up. But pity anyone who falls and has no one to help them

7. Ecclesiastes 4:7–8.

up."[8] A whole lot of people these days are lying emotionally helpless on the roadside, alone.

It drains us. Sustaining a protective force field around our hearts requires enormous amounts of personal energy. It's tiring. Israel's great but deeply flawed king, David, wrote of the weariness he endured attempting to hide his true condition: "When I kept silent, my bones wasted away through my groaning all day long."[9] Eventually our vitality taps out and we have little left to offer anyone, including ourselves.

It hardens us. Mistrust calcifies our hearts, hardening into cynicism and skepticism. We assume impure motives in people. My brother Mark (who shares my taste for fine sarcasm) and I often repeat a phrase when bemoaning how people consistently let us down: "The only two people I trust in this world are you and me. And sometimes I wonder about you." We're only half joking when we say it. Distancing our true selves from others amplifies a jaded view of the world, fueling impatience, anger, judgmentalism, and superiority.

It weakens our self-awareness. The more we hide our true condition from others, the more difficult it becomes to perceive it ourselves. The act of revealing our authentic selves to others also serves to mirror them back to us. When the mirror is removed, our capacity to notice what the reflection might expose diminishes.

It pressurizes our issues. The secrets of the heart are combustive. The more they're concentrated, the more explosive they become. A containment strategy is impossible to maintain permanently and only makes the inevitable revelation of a dark secret more destructive. "You can't keep your true self hidden forever," Jesus said. "Before long you'll be exposed."[10]

8. Ecclesiastes 4:10.   9. Psalm 32:3.   10. Luke 12:2 MSG.

I have seen more than one small group environment where a couple never hinted that their marriage was struggling until they announced their impending divorce to their shocked and devastated friends. The first time many people become aware of a family member's trouble with alcohol is when they learn of a DUI arrest. The longer personal issues, addictions, and impure habits remain hidden, the broader the blast and the farther the shrapnel flies when the bomb inevitably detonates. If we wait until the threat reaches DEFCON 1 before sounding the alarm, the missiles may already be flying.

It deadens us. Our emotional state is inherently linked to our soul's health.[c] When we seal off our hearts from others, we also numb our capacity to care, to enter fully into another's joys or sorrows. We become increasingly desensitized— less capable of experiencing true delight, sympathy, passion, or hope.

How many of these effects have you noticed in your own heart?

The Doorway to "Life"

Liberation from these effects, if we really want it, begins at the same place for us as it did for our first parents. Though he knew exactly where Adam was concealed, "the LORD God called to the man, 'Where are you?'"[11]—standing ready to offer a covering for Adam and Eve's nakedness if they would simply step into the clearing and expose their true condition.

God's invitation to us is the same as it was to them: Stop hiding. Show yourself as you are. Present your true state. The coverings God fashioned for Adam and his wife in the

11. Genesis 3:9.

38

garden weren't given to hide their true condition. They were provided to cover their shame. To restore their dignity *in the midst of* their imperfection.

The path to that restoration begins with opening our hearts rather than concealing them, presenting our true selves rather than masking them. Listen as Jesus tells it straight: "Everyone who does evil hates the light, and will not come into the light for fear that their deeds will be exposed. But whoever lives by the truth comes into the light, so that it may be seen plainly that what they have done has been done in the sight of God."[12]

This is and always has been the path to setting our souls free—radically unearthing their true condition, then declaring to the Redeemer something like this:

> *I'm done self-justifying and self-protecting. I'm done playing the victim. I'm done trying to prove my own worth. I'm done building myself up in others' minds or in my own. I'm not just done; I'm "undone."*[13] *I admit to everything: my impotence, my degeneracy, my desolation. I offer no defense; I'm guilty of it all. I'm not "coming clean," I'm coming dirty. I'm incapable of producing anything righteous, whole, or pure. I'm laying myself bare.*

What would a similar declaration look like for you?

This is where our heart's restoration begins. But it's not where it ends. Simply bringing a defective heart into the open doesn't effect change on it any more than incising a surgical patient cures their disease. The exposed soul must be acted upon by an outside agent—something capable of generating healing when brought into contact.

12. John 3:20–21.   13. Isaiah 6:5 KJV.

That something is the gospel—the love-drenched, grace-driven, soul-reanimating gift of utter acceptance and irrevocable restoration, paid for in blood by Christ at the cross and delivered in power at his resurrection. When the corrupted soul is lifted in dependent surrender to the gospel's touch, God does for it what no other force in the universe can do. He saturates it with his absolute cleansing and forgiveness. He revives it with his energizing life force. He embraces it with his tender affection. He "restores my soul."[14]

Your heart needs the gospel.

If about now you're saying, "Right. I know this. I've given my heart to Christ; I've received the gift of eternal life. We can move on," it's crucial that you don't. This conscious connection of your broken spirit to its restorer isn't just the one-time act of regeneration. *It's also the delivery system for ongoing doses of the gospel's reanimating effect on your soul.* It's not just the way *to* salvation; it is the way *of* salvation. We consistently need the gospel. To refresh our exposure to it. To consistently bring our exposed hearts back to its rejuvenating vitality. To submerge our souls in its restorative waters. Every. Single. Day.

When we realize that the gospel-touched soul is always the nucleus for any substantive change we want to see within ourselves, it's worth our while to look a bit closer at how exactly our souls work and how we work with them. What we discover next may profoundly alter the way we approach our heart's transformation.

14. Psalm 23:3 ESV.

3

Anatomy of an Open Soul

If you've ever participated in a school choir or taken vocal lessons, you're probably familiar with the directive to sing "from the diaphragm." The diaphragm is the large muscle sheath spanning the bottom of the rib cage that, when properly engaged, helps drive air forcefully and consistently from the lungs toward the vocal cords.

At least, that's the theory. Most of us in the choir had no idea we even possessed such a thing, much less where to find it or how to sing from it.

Something similar can be true when we hear Scripture say that the *zoé*-level aliveness and relationships we were made for are directly related to opening and engaging our souls. While we may have heard a lot about the soul and its importance, we may also have little clue what it is, where it is, or how to affect any substantive change on it.

And that's why it's worth taking time for a brief anatomy lesson to understand how the Bible describes the soul's

41

design and function and, more importantly, the means by which it is transformed.

Our Superior Superpower

People like to debate which of the superpowers they see in the movies are the greatest or which one they'd possess if they could choose, but as human beings, we've already been bestowed with something even greater than the ability to fly or time travel. When God breathed a "soul"[a] into the first man and woman, he endowed them with something no other entity in creation had been given. Our souls not only serve as the seat of our identity, motives, and beliefs but they also contain a "God gene" that enables us to mirror[b] some of the Almighty's exclusive qualities: the power to create, the capacity to be self-aware, the ability to reason, the volition to choose. Animals didn't get that. Angels didn't get that. But Adam and Eve got it. And so did we.

But God didn't stop there. He also equipped us with instruments and systems that connect to and extend from our souls: Intellect. Emotion. Corporal activity. These aren't siloed, independently functioning entities, nor are they the

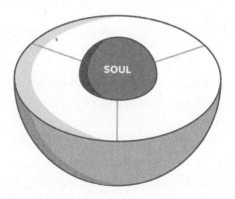

soul itself. Rather, they serve as vehicles that extend naturally from our soul and interact with our world.

Scripture uses a variety of terms to identify and describe these components: spirit, mind, strength, heart, and others. They so intertwine in their connection with each other and the soul that, when the Bible lists them together in significant passages such as the Shema of Deuteronomy 6 ("Love the LORD your God with all your heart and with all your soul and with all your strength"[1]) and the "Great Commandment" in the Gospels ("Love the Lord your God with all your heart and with all your soul and with all your mind"[2]), it varies their order and number, and occasionally uses them interchangeably.[c]

Everything you do as a human being—every choice, action, attitude, and feeling—channels through some combination of these components. You walk around exercising your five senses, thinking and emoting, deciding and interacting. You choose which passions and priorities you'll pursue; what and how and to whom you'll speak; whom you'll marry and how you'll parent; where you'll reside, work, and play; which

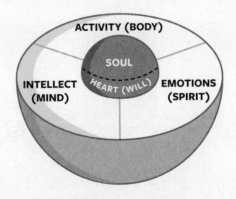

1. Deuteronomy 6:5. 2. Matthew 22:37; see also Mark 12:30; Luke 10:27.

locales you'll frequent and what behaviors you'll exhibit in them; and the degree to which you'll follow God's instructions while you're living the life you've been gifted.

Because our minds, emotions, and actions are all intrinsic parts of who we are, we rightfully recognize that they're also integrally involved in any movement we might pursue toward spiritual health and growth. And this is where it gets interesting.

The Outside-In Approach

Most typical approaches to spiritual growth focus on one or more of these soul-extending channels as the starting point for change. They introduce sets of practices, habits, experiences, and influences designed to retrench our thinking, reshape our behaviors, and reorient our drives. The mix can include spiritual disciplines such as prayer and Scripture reading, kingdom service, community and accountability, worship participation, and sacrificial giving, which presumably combine to penetrate the character and renovate the heart.

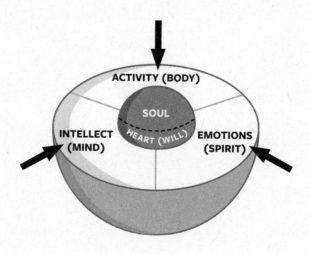

Such efforts often generate noticeable, tangible results. But they also carry an inherent risk: they can be fully implemented and successfully executed without necessarily affecting the soul. Even the best discipleship programs can prove powerless to produce internal transformation, because it's possible to consistently and meticulously maintain respected spiritual practices and never engage the heart at all.[d] Summarized as a principle: behavior modification alone doesn't change character. Expressed in common parlance: you can put lipstick on a pig, but it's still a pig.[e]

Scripture's statements to this effect are pointed and dramatic:

- God proclaimed through Jeremiah, "Your burnt offerings are not acceptable; your sacrifices do not please me."[3]
- Ezekiel declared, "Their mouths speak of love, but their hearts are greedy for unjust gain."[4]
- The apostle Paul warned the Colossians that some who practiced spiritual disciplines "indeed have an appearance of wisdom, with their self-imposed worship, their false humility and their harsh treatment of the body, but they lack any value in restraining sensual indulgence."[5]
- Jesus told some of the most externally obedient moralists in his audience, "You clean the outside of the cup and dish, but inside [you] are full of greed and self-indulgence."[6]
- He reinforced the message with these blunt words: "You are like whitewashed tombs, which look beautiful on the outside but on the inside are full of the

3. Jeremiah 6:20.   4. Ezekiel 33:31.   5. Colossians 2:23.   6. Matthew 23:25.

bones of the dead and everything unclean. In the same way, on the outside you appear to people as righteous but on the inside you are full of hypocrisy and wickedness."[7]

- In perhaps his most chilling statement, Christ foretold that at the last judgment some will say, "Did we not prophesy in your name and in your name drive out demons and in your name perform many miracles?" and he said he would "tell them plainly, 'I never knew you. Away from me, you evildoers!'"[8]

What all this means in real-life terms is that it's possible for someone to acknowledge God, praise him, pray to him, serve him, master his Word, and obey his instructions—but do so from an unopened, disconnected soul, which can leave the heart not only unchanged but hardened and proud.

You've witnessed this. Chances are, some of the most un-Christlike people you've met are also among the most biblically knowledgeable. Some of the harshest, most graceless, judgmental individuals in your life may also be those who seldom miss a Sunday service or church program. Some of the people exposed as hiding the darkest sin habits are also those you've watched pray most eloquently, tithe most generously, serve most faithfully, and lead most dynamically.

Perhaps a face or two popped into your mind as you read that last paragraph. Perhaps the face is your own. Our efforts to pursue spiritual activity can be well-intentioned, but unless something has first been activated within our soul, they produce only reformation, not transformation.

7. Matthew 23:27–28.   8. Matthew 7:22–23.

"Engage Your Core"

During my doomed-from-the-start attempt to attain so-called abs of steel, my personal trainer observed that the exercises I was using were fine, but my technique was all wrong. He said I needed to "engage my core" when attempting the dreaded crunches, mountain climbers, and dead bugs. It was possible, I was told, to go through the external motions without activating my core while doing so.

I immediately noticed the difference. Engaging my core required deliberate focus on that area, intentional isolation and activation of the muscle group I wanted to develop. I realized why I hadn't done so before. It was harder work. I didn't like it. So I stopped.

I never attained an eight-pack, six-pack, or any pack for that matter, but I did learn that there's a big difference between performing the mechanics of an exercise and engaging the actual muscle.

The process for enacting true, life-giving transformation follows a similar pattern—one that can be summarized in a simple but fundamental principle: Don't start with your head. Don't start with your hands. Start with your heart.

The Bible has repeated the message across generations:

- "Circumcise your hearts."[9]
- "Rend your heart and not your garments."[10]
- "You will seek me and find me when you seek me with all your heart."[11]
- "Search me, God, and know my heart."[12]

9. Deuteronomy 10:16.   10. Joel 2:13.   11. Jeremiah 29:13.   12. Psalm 139:23.

- "First clean the inside of the cup and dish, and then the outside also will be clean."[13]
- "My sacrifice, O God, is a broken spirit; a broken and contrite heart you, God, will not despise."[14]

Putting this into practice is far more rare than it should be. But the means of initiating it is thankfully not complicated. It begins when we intentionally stop to identify our heart and bring it, opened and unguarded, into direct contact with God in a personal, relationally intimate presentation of our truest self. It's something you can enact at this very moment. Allow me to suggest an exercise to do just that—right here, right now.

Pause where you are. I genuinely encourage you not just to read the next several lines but to tangibly enact them. Look around the room you're sitting in and consciously become aware that Christ is actually, literally present in the room with you. He's near you, close enough to touch. He's completely and fully aware of everything you're holding inside your true self. He knows the thoughts you had a half hour ago, the temptations you indulged in this week, the impulses you gave in to this year. He knows the ugly motives you're hiding, the resentments you're harboring, the attitudes you're festering. He knows the lines you cross, the standards you compromise, the fantasies you entertain in the dark. He knows what you say, what you do, what you think. He knows the wounds you carry, the abuses you've suffered, the betrayals you've endured. He knows your weakness, your shame, your fear, your doubt. The truest you. He knows it all.

13. Matthew 23:26.   14. Psalm 51:17.

Next, consciously incline that truest self—your heart, exactly as it is—toward him. Turn to face him. Show yourself to him. Everything laid bare. No explanations, no excuses. Reveal it all to him and acknowledge that he sees it—all of it. Do so in humility and as an act of unqualified, full surrender. Open your empty hands toward him if it helps. Even if you don't say anything, simply lay your will and your heart in front of him. Submit your soul to him, to do with it as he sees fit.

Now, with the eyes of your heart, envision his response. See his face as he looks at you with absolute love. Feel his compassion and forgiveness as he moves toward you with intimacy and affection. Watch him gently take your heart, even in its ugliest current state, and hold it as if it's the most precious possession in the universe. Watch him breathe his Spirit on it. Watch him apply his own purity to it. Watch him hold it out to you again, cleansed and accepted, purified and restored, handing it back to you knowing he has placed his own heart within it.

Then hear his voice as he gently and tenderly says something like this: "Yes, you're flawed, marred, broken at your very core. Yes, I know everything, and I see completely who and what you are. But you are now wrapped in my love. You're now drenched in my forgiveness. You're saturated by my purity. You are granted full pardon and absolution. You belong to me. In this moment, in every moment, you are beloved, cherished, and secure. Your acceptance is complete. Your position is absolute. Your worth is permanent. You are whole."

This is the epicenter of true transformation. This is where the ability to live from an open soul begins.

The Inside-Out Alternative

When our first step is direct action on our core self, the proper order for meaningful connection with our world is enacted. Transformation happens from the inside out. God pours *zoé* into our surrendered heart, resets it, reidentifies it, and cleanses it. He then energizes it so that it can turn toward its world with health and wholeness and *choose to remain open*. Its vibrancy radically alters every channel through which it manifests itself: the will's choices, the body's activities, the intellect's thinking, the emotion's expressions and communications.

Here, then, is the progression that produces the fullest, richest inward life, which in turn forms the seedbed for growing meaningful, heart-level connection with others:

- start with your heart
- identify your heart
- open your heart
- expose your heart

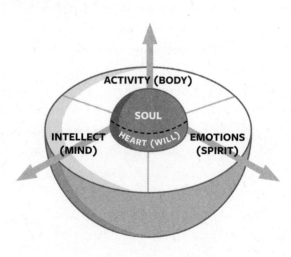

- activate your heart
- submit your heart
- receive God's transformation on your heart

Once you establish this foundation, you'll be ready to move toward presenting an open soul to others.

Then hang on tight, because the first person you need to do that with is someone very close to you.

4

Getting Honest with Yourself

The Neverending Story, Michael Ende's fantasy novel about a world threatened by humanity's disappearing imagination, follows the hero, Atreyu, as he faces a series of gates that test his character. The most difficult is the Magic Mirror Gate, which forces the one who gazes into it to encounter their "real innermost self."[a]

In the film adaptation, upon hearing of the mirror's power, Falkor the Luck Dragon says, "That won't be too hard."

"That's what everyone thinks," comes the reply from Engywook, watcher of the gate. "But kind people find out that they are cruel. Brave men discover that they are really cowards. Confronted by their true selves, most men run away screaming!"[b]

If we aspire to live in Level 3 honesty, the first and most difficult person to do it with might be the one we see looking back at us in the mirror. "Don't think you are better than you really are," the apostle Paul wrote. "Be honest in your evaluation of yourselves."[1] He joined Jesus in instructing believers to take a good, hard look at themselves even before participating in spiritual activities like worship and communion.[2] And should we choose to look in that mirror, we'll be confronted with a dirty little secret we carry everywhere we go: we lie to ourselves.

That statement may raise your hackles, but we must understand that dishonesty with oneself is so universal, most of us are oblivious to it . . . even while we're doing it. The lies can take a variety of forms, but a handful stand out among the most commonly practiced and finely tuned. As we stop here for a moment to look into this mirror, resist the urge to run away.

Self-Delusion

Self-delusion arises out of a desire to believe something about ourselves that simply isn't true. We embellish our accomplishments and skill levels to stack up favorably in a world that measures personal value on the basis of performance and comparison to others.

The delusion is usually obvious . . . to everyone except ourselves. Singing competition contestants routinely insist their voices have been compared to Mariah Carey or Celine Dion. Sixty-five percent of the population claims to be above average in intelligence.[c] Nearly a third of adult American males genuinely believe they could have gone pro in their high school sport if one or two breaks had gone differently.[d]

You may have already waved off those examples as ridiculous. You're far too self-aware to believe such absurdities. But

1. Romans 12:3 NLT.   2. Matthew 5:23–24.

don't kid yourself. Self-delusion is almost certainly active within you in one form or another.

Still don't think so? Here's a question for you: Do you look your age? Seventy-five percent of adults over thirty believe they look younger than their contemporaries.[e] Do the math and let that sink in. "Now hang on a minute," you say, "people actually tell me that all the time. They go on and on about it." Yes . . . and they're lying. They're just trying to be polite.

The hard truth is that you *do* look your age, you *don't* turn heads with your breathtaking good looks, you're fairly average in intelligence and skills, and you occasionally emit some unpleasant odors.

Self-Deception

If self-delusion is wanting to believe something about ourselves that is *not* true, self-deception is choosing not to believe something about ourselves that *is* true. We employ revisionist history to cast ourselves as victims rather than culprits while recounting uncomfortable moments. We edit our recollection of tense exchanges when we said something awful or did something inappropriate that exposed our dark side. We spin-doctor the story to diminish certain incriminating details, attaching responsibility-skirting phrases to these altered memories:

- "I didn't mean it that way."
- "I was just trying to help."
- "I was provoked."
- "Someone else started it."
- "I was young and didn't know any better."

- "I had no choice."
- "It wasn't a big deal."

There's a reason Scripture speaks often of Christ followers' propensity for self-deception. It seems we're naturals at it. But God's Word grabs us by the nape of the neck and ushers us back to the mirror. "If anyone thinks they are something when they are not," Paul tells the Galatians, "they deceive themselves."[3]

Self-Denial

This might be the most common way we lie to ourselves. We endure mistreatment or perceived wrongdoing, say it's forgotten and in the past, but harbor resentments and personal grudges that affect our future attitudes and dealings.

We talk and act as if we're not affected by the injury long-term, but we're like the Black Knight whose arms have been cut off in *Monty Python and the Holy Grail*, proclaiming, "'Tis but a scratch . . . just a flesh wound."[f] The truth bleeds out in ways others can see but that we think we're successfully masking: passive-aggressive behaviors, nonverbal expressions of displeasure, withdrawal from relationship and strategic avoidance of the person against whom we carry the grudge. We maintain that we're above pettiness and bitterness but secretly feel pleasure when we hear of negative things happening to the one who hurt us. If we're ever asked for our thoughts about the situation, we insist it's ancient history with no lingering effects, but our responses are reminiscent of Jeremiah's words, "'Peace, peace,' they say, when there is no peace."[4]

3. Galatians 6:3.   4. Jeremiah 6:14.

Self-Diversion

Like ignoring the dashboard warning lights in our car, our easiest option is to simply avoid introspection altogether. We busy our lives with commitments and activities, flooding our senses with screen time and binge-watching to keep ourselves occupied, conveniently running out of time to ever inspect our soul's condition. We instinctively know we wouldn't like what we'd see if we investigated the deeper corners of our hearts, so we ignore any noise or stench occasionally emanating outward. Whatever shiny object might be nearby easily diverts our attention, and we happily chase it in the opposite direction of the hard realities festering within our souls.

It's no surprise that James, the brother of Jesus, also used a mirror metaphor when he described the one who sees the truth God's Word reveals and, "after looking at himself, goes away and immediately forgets what he looks like."[5] We can convince ourselves there's nothing in the reflection worth seeing, nothing in our hearts producing any adverse effect. We figure the dashboard light will eventually turn itself off.

Self-delusion, self-deception, self-denial, self-diversion. Do a quick, honest self-assessment: Which ones show up most in your own reflection?

Three Liberating Self-Admissions

Living from a fully honest soul begins with telling the truth *to* ourselves, *about* ourselves. The truth that we're flawed, marred, and inadequate. The truth that we're nothing

5. James 1:24.

without the gospel's soul-saturating forgiveness and freedom. And the truth of the following trio of declarations, which may feel a bit jarring at first but will, if fully internalized, go a long way toward liberating us from the inside out.

1. **I'm not special, and I don't need to be.** Many of us have spent our whole lives feeling pressured to prove our worth by establishing ourselves as distinct. Superior. Extraordinary. What C. S. Lewis called "the great sin"[g]— our personal pride—has driven us to convince ourselves and others around us that we've accomplished what others haven't and possess qualities that others don't. We're stronger, smarter, more committed, more gifted. We're kind of a big deal. All the while we walk around terrified at the prospect of being exposed as simply run-of-the-mill, typical, or—heaven forbid—inferior.

But the gospel's liberating embrace allows our opened hearts to find our worth outside of our performance or comparison to others. And it releases us to willingly acknowledge, and be at complete peace with, what our deepest soul already knows to be true: we're not special. Sure, as human beings we exist as the crowning achievement of all creation, image bearers of God who are "fearfully and wonderfully made."[6] But among our fellow image bearers, we're no more special than anyone else. We're not one in a million; we're merely one *of* a million . . . or, more accurately, of eight billion. The writer of Ecclesiastes calls it the fate of all humankind to live largely unremarkable lives and be quickly forgotten once we die.[7] The more readily we accept that, the healthier our hearts become.

6. Psalm 139:14.   7. Ecclesiastes 1:11; 9:5.

When my daughter decided to take a postcollege, gap year tour of Europe, I immediately insisted she watch every *Taken* movie ever made—the premise of which is a single daughter who is abducted and trafficked while traveling abroad before her hero father comes to her rescue and dispenses justice to her captors. I then went to great lengths to make my daughter aware of one supremely important fact: her father (me) is not Liam Neeson, nor does he possess "a very particular set of skills" that would enable him to declare with absolute certainty to any potential assailant, "I will find you, and I will kill you."[h]

I wanted to make that point abundantly clear so that she would take extra precautions for her own safety. Sure, I *wish* I possessed the kinds of skills they make movies about. But in reality, I'm a regular, unexceptional, entirely ordinary man, capable of little more than working, loving imperfectly, and cracking a dad joke now and then. And that truth holds true in pretty much every situation I find myself in and with every group I'm a part of. I'm completely average at most things, decent at a few, and downright awful at plenty more. I'm going to assume the same is true of you.

Can you be okay with that?

I believe you can, for this reason: the God who designed you has declared unequivocally that it's not your gifts and abilities, accomplishments, or drive that make you worthwhile. It's his enveloping righteousness, provided freely by his Son. No one, absolutely no one, is more worthy than you, nor is anyone less worthy. Hear him say it through his Word and by his Spirit, not just to the world at large but directly to your individual soul. You don't have to be "special." You only need to be his.

2. **I'm not innocent, and I don't need to pretend I am.**
Here's the hard-to-swallow pill you may be surprised to discover won't poison you: at your true core, you're not only no
better than anyone else around you but you're every bit as
flawed as the worst of them. Every bit as guilty, every bit as
capable of horrible thoughts and compromised standards.
You may be forgiven, but you're not innocent.

It can be daunting to admit to ourselves that we actually
did intend to wound with the terrible words we said; we
were indeed responsible for that hurtful act; we are in fact
harboring resentment toward that person. Some of us have
made excuses for just about every misdeed we've ever committed. Some are doing it at this very moment.

But heart-level honesty with yourself means accepting full
responsibility for your actions, words, and motives. If you were
there, say so. If you entertained that evil thought, stiffen your
back and admit the truth. If you broke that commandment,
harbored those ill feelings, or betrayed that trust, don't ratio-
nalize it, minimize it, or excuse it any longer. Come clean in
self-confession. Own it. The point isn't to sensationalize your
guilt or wallow in self-loathing; it's to open your heart to honest self-admission and repentance and then feel the warm wave
of God's unconditional forgiveness sweep over you and declare
you restored and secure. As pastor and author Timothy Keller
said, "We are more sinful and flawed in ourselves than we ever
dared believe, yet at the very same time we are more loved and
accepted in Jesus Christ than we ever dared hope."[i]

Theologian Martin Luther is famously quoted as saying
believers should sin boldly. Many have argued over his meaning, but at minimum, it points to God's grace as so powerful,
we need not hide the sins we knowingly commit. We can own

up to them "boldly" because they provide the dark backdrop against which grace's vivid colors are displayed on our soul's canvas. We shouldn't be proud of our sins, but we should accept full responsibility for them. Because when we do, the cross bursts through, dispensing a grace that vaporizes our guilt and shame. Paul said as much in Romans 5:20–21: "But where sin increased, grace increased all the more, so that, just as sin reigned in death, so also grace might reign through righteousness to bring eternal life through Jesus Christ our Lord."

Acknowledging our agency in the sins we commit activates and amplifies the kind of humility that can alter a soul's condition. Softening it. Gentling it. Making it absorbent to a God-generated grace that then transforms it—what Scripture calls exchanging a heart of stone for one of flesh.[8]

Speak that truth in your own heart and know that as a believer you're not defined by your sin or on the hook for its punishment, because its penalty has long been paid. Wear your redemption in full view so the world can be stunned by grace's liberating power.

3. **I'm not unscarred, and I don't need to convince myself that I am.** Hannah Hurnard's classic allegory of the Christian life, *Hinds' Feet on High Places*, follows the main character, Much-Afraid, on her quest to find the shepherd's High Places. For her journey, Much-Afraid is assigned two companions—Sorrow and Suffering—and she's instructed to hold their hands every step of the way.[j]

The same two companions accompany you on your trek through a fallen world. Your heart sustains trauma and injury, unmet longing and deep wounding. Tribulations pummel every Christ follower, regardless of how devout they

8. Ezekiel 11:19.

are. Recognizing the effect their sustained blows have on your soul is an essential part of living out an open-hearted honesty with yourself.

A misguided notion sometimes creeps into Christian circles. It sometimes parades under the banner of Victorious Christian Living and suggests that to acknowledge the influence, or even the presence, of pain and injury in our souls is to admit a lack of trust in the God who always prevails, who works all things together for the good of those who love him.[9] We're compelled to muster up a brave face, will ourselves into believing we are unmoved, and declare we will not be daunted by that which is trying, to borrow a common Christian catchphrase, to "rob us of our joy."

But not only does that mentality find little support in Scripture, it also stands contrary to the Bible's principles for walking in honest connection with God. The psalms of lament repeatedly model acknowledging, bearing, and even lingering in the soul's anguish. In them David exposes his true condition to his heavenly Father, revealing he carries sorrow in his heart "day after day."[10] Rather than downplay their presence, he declares, "My problems go from bad to worse."[11]

Listen to Psalm 31:

> I am in distress;
>> my eyes grow weak with sorrow,
>> my soul and body with grief.
> My life is consumed by anguish
>> and my years by groaning;
>> my strength fails because of my affliction,
>> and my bones grow weak.[12]

9. Romans 8:28.   10. Psalm 13:2.   11. Psalm 25:17 NLT.   12. Psalm 31:9–10.

Those don't sound like the joyful chants of someone naming and claiming victory over heartache. They're honest reflections of the soul's true condition, freely expressed to One still being trusted to deliver in the end.

God can handle your honesty. He invites it. He encourages it.

The same Paul who wrote that he "delight[ed]" in what his sufferings signified also confessed that he "despaired" in the middle of them, even to the point of fearing they would kill him.[13] The language of 2 Corinthians 12 indicates Paul so valued what God was accomplishing through the pain that he accepted it willingly, with a sense of gratitude. He didn't look for quick fixes or deny that it caused him so much internal torment that he repeatedly begged for its removal.

Faith is not incompatible with anguish. They coexist in the fully honest soul. We feel negative emotions. We struggle and ache. We're not capable of taking everything in stride. We're not at complete peace with everything we're experiencing. Acknowledging and expressing those realities are marks of an honest, softened heart, not a faithless one.

Pretense is the enemy of an open soul. God doesn't want us to deny who we are or what we feel; he wants us to be active participators in our frailty. He not only allows us to experience soul weakness, he invites us to sit in its heartache, permitting it to increase our longing for a balm only he can provide *in the midst* of the pain, not *in place* of it.

───────

When these liberating declarations are consciously made and fully embraced, they unlock a level of aliveness beyond

13. 2 Corinthians 12:10; 1:8.

anything we may have experienced before. The resulting vitality opens a new channel in the way we move toward others—one that can revolutionize the health and vibrancy of our personal relationships. And that's where we're headed next.

5

What It Takes to Live Open-Hearted with Others

Now it gets real.

It's one thing to move toward heart-open, Level 3 honesty with yourself or, for that matter, with God.[a] Those are "internal" relationships, not exposed socially or witnessed publicly. It's quite another to live open-souled with other walking, talking humans—people who make snap judgments and form unwarranted opinions, who post gossip on social media and can directly affect your reputation, your relationships, even your livelihood.

As we discussed earlier, *people* let us down. *People* betray each other. *People* can't be trusted. The Miranda warning may have been written for criminals, but it can be applied to virtually all human relationships: "Anything you say can and will be used against you." Heart-open honesty with others can bite you in the backside.

You need it anyway.

God puts it front and center in the church's function. He prescribes specific instructions to ensure its proper practice, repeatedly directing his people to treat it as a nonnegotiable. It's healthy, right, and good.

It also runs contrary to pretty much every natural impulse, which means it requires intentionality and deliberate implementation. And that puts open-hearted living with others in the same category as skydiving or having a colonoscopy—it might turn out to be a great decision, but no one's ever going to be able to force you into it.

Once you decide it's worth doing, though, three defining activators serve to kick it into motion.

The Full Disclosure Part

Open-hearted living with others begins with a straightforward decision—to offer others a full, unobstructed view of our current condition. To say, "Okay, this is me, the true me. Unedited. Unfiltered."

Sounds simple enough. Jesus did it with Peter, James, and John in Gethsemane.[b] The Psalms commend the one who "speaks the truth from their heart."[1] But it's something most of us have seldom seen and rarely practice. We become so accustomed to providing only vague details of our lives and situations, we're not even aware we're allowing others limited access to the most pertinent facts.

My work leading spiritual formation cohorts utilizes a series of retreats and exercises designed to cultivate authentic, heart-to-heart interaction. On one occasion a participant

1. Psalm 15:2.

who wasn't able to attend one of the gatherings sent a group email apologizing for his absence, indicating some "personal issues" had kept him away. He then sent me a second, individual message detailing an illness requiring a hospital stay, compounded by a grueling work situation, plus an unwarranted personal attack. It sounded awful.

I was grateful to better know how to pray for him, but I also wondered why he felt the need to send two different versions of the story, especially given the group's express purpose to create a safe haven for each other's souls. When I asked, his reply was telling. He said he had no earthly idea. He concluded it was "just force of habit." Viewing the group as an environment where he could reveal everything he was going through hadn't even crossed his mind. After our exchange he changed course and sent the second email to the entire cohort. He instantly received a tremendous amount of prayer, support, and personal encouragement.

It raises a question. If Galatians 6:2 and Romans 12:15 aren't just flowery language, how can we "carry each other's burdens" if those burdens are never disclosed? How can we "rejoice with those who rejoice, and weep with those who weep"[2] unless the rejoicing's and weeping's core causes are revealed?

I'll ask it a bit more directly. When was the last time you raised a loud, spontaneous cheer with someone over their good news or personal accomplishment? (Your kid's goofy performance in the school play doesn't count.) When was the last time you shed actual, physical tears with another over something one of you was enduring? Think specifically—the people living next door, the ones you work alongside, those with whom you serve and worship at church. Do you know

2. NKJV.

what they're really going through this week? The heaviest weights they're currently carrying? The issues robbing them of sleep right now? Do they know yours?

Offering full disclosure to others creates a breeding ground for meaningful guidance, strengthened bonds of friendship, and levels of encouragement and support you may have longed for but never received. As author Henry Cloud said in his definitive work *Changes That Heal*, "It is literally never too late to open up to those who love us and care about our development. . . . God can use our current relationships to provide the nurturing we didn't receive as children, the mentoring we missed as school-age kids, or the companionship we needed as teenagers."[c]

Again, this kind of exposure doesn't happen without a conscious decision: to bring your genuine, true condition into another's field of vision. But the good news is that once you start, the longer you do it, the easier it gets. It's like finally losing the toupee or throwing away the hair coloring. There may be initial shock, but it subsides quickly and the natural state soon feels liberatingly normal.

The True Confessions Part

Here's where it really gets down and dirty.

You have skeletons in your closet—elements of your past you're neither proud of nor like to think about. You've convinced yourself they're ancient history, irrelevant, appropriately and permanently buried. You can't imagine a scenario in which you would ever disclose them of your own volition.

You also hold other pockets of darkness—present and active involvements, thoughts, and habits. You're fighting them—sometimes successfully, sometimes not. One or two could cause significant damage if they ever saw the light of day.

Then there are current, so-called "small" indiscretions and areas of weakness that creep into and out of your life. Matters of temper and gossip, greed and selfishness, over-indulgence and vulnerability to temptation. They're part of being human—frustrating but "managed."

This collection occupies a hidden space within your heart, as it does in everyone's. According to one study, "ninety-seven percent of people are keeping a significant secret at any given time, with the average person having about 13 secrets."[d] They may not all fall into the category of "sin," but you're very aware of the ones that do. You've confessed them to God, worked hard to overcome their effects, and guarded against their recurrence. And you keep them to yourself.

And then you read a little passage tucked away in the epistle of James. It relates to how we engage with others in the family of God and simply says, "Confess your sins to each other."[3]

Oh, you've dipped your toe in that water before. You've acknowledged your general sinfulness with statements like, "I admit it, I'm not perfect. I'm a sinner" (i.e., Level 1 honesty). You've occasionally even delved into some below-the-surface confession where you've announced, "Here are some specific ways I've blown it in the past" (i.e., Level 2 honesty). But now you're faced with the prospect of living fully open-hearted, which presumably includes exposing the parts you've worked so hard to ignore (or forget) to the view of select others who weren't involved in or affected by those choices.

Is that really necessary? What good can come from revealing your dark history and private offenses to those who

3. James 5:16.

hold no authority as judges over them, nor any capacity to do anything constructive about them? The answer may go a long way toward explaining why even Christian relationships so often remain shallow: undisclosed sin acts as an intimacy inhibitor within the soul.

Forgiveness and cleansing may have been received from God, but sin, if left unrevealed to others, leaves residual contaminants within our hearts that naturally isolate themselves from exposure. They prompt avoidance of interactions that could risk revealing their presence and ongoing impact. Emotional distance results, making it more difficult for others to know us fully, connect with us deeply, and love us effectually. The book of Hebrews speaks of hidden sin's calcifying effect, which can eventually form a deceitful crust over the human heart.[4] The longer we leave our sins undivulged, the thicker and harder the callous can grow.

No soul should leave sin's remnant concealed. No one should ever die with a secret.

God utilizes three primary instruments to counter the effects of sin's residual infection in the believer's heart: his Word, his Spirit, and his people channeling his grace and truth to one another. The first two tend to get the most press. But the third carries a distinct potency. Soul-level connectivity, where we expose the dark recesses of our condition to each other, allows God's Spirit residing within us to deliver his strength, wisdom, and continued cleansing directly into one another's hearts.

Please read that last sentence again. Allow it to soak in. Notice: we don't generate that cleansing; we simply serve as a conduit through which God's Spirit pours grace into each other's souls. Heart-level confession opens the conduit.[e]

4. Hebrews 3:12–13.

The old Scottish proverb "Confession is good for the soul" is profoundly true. But confession isn't solely a vertical act; it's also a horizontal one. Twelve-step recovery groups have long recognized this component of the Bible's prescription and incorporated it into their programs. It's a big reason why they're as successful as they are. Every Christ follower needs the same outlet, where the darkest parts of the true self are honestly exposed to God's grace-agents.

Do those you endeavor to live open-hearted toward need to know about the indiscretion early in your marriage, the occasional relapses into pornography, the tendency to overspend, the occasional outbursts of temper? No, they don't. And yes, they do. When voluntarily offered, Level 3 disclosure of our sins—both small and large, past and present—opens the door of our hearts to transformative doses of understanding, support, guidance, and grace. As author Ann Voskamp has said, "Shame dies when stories are told in safe places."[f]

So allow me to ask directly: What secrets—the ones you've decided are best taken to your grave—are you still carrying? To whom might you unlock the door they're hiding behind in order to neutralize their toxins? Do you have people with whom you share a pact to initiate consistent, uncomfortable check-ins to reveal not just your past secrets but your current temptations and recent sins? If not, who could you invite to be the first?

The Teachable Spirit Part

The test for whether someone has fully opened their heart to another isn't how much or how quickly they divulge their secrets but how willingly they receive input once they have.

A truly exposed soul doesn't just speak, it listens. It invites candid feedback and presents a teachable spirit that's receptive to learning how to move toward health and growth. I may open the floodgates and pour out all my woes in the name of being honest and vulnerable, but if I'm telling the same sad story over and over—never working through it or able to move past it—the act becomes self-indulgent. Airing one's dirty laundry without sincerely seeking a way to clean it serves only to draw attention to oneself, gain sympathy, or dominate discussion. That isn't authenticity; it's manipulation.

Full, open-souled disclosure includes an earnest request for godly perspective, guidance, and, at times, firm correction. It's where Scripture's renowned proverb is lived out: "As iron sharpens iron, so one person sharpens another."[5] And the book of Proverbs seemingly can't emphasize this point enough:

- "Whoever hates correction is stupid."[6]
- "Whoever heeds correction is honored."[7]
- "Whoever heeds correction shows prudence."[8]
- "Whoever heeds life-giving correction will be at home among the wise. . . . The one who heeds correction gains understanding."[9]
- "Listen to advice and accept discipline, and at the end you will be counted among the wise."[10]

A heart fully opening itself to others brings with it a genuine invitation: *Tell me the truth. Point out what you see. Tag*

5. Proverbs 27:17.   6. Proverbs 12:1.   7. Proverbs 13:18.   8. Proverbs 15:5.
9. Proverbs 15:31–32.   10. Proverbs 19:20.

*me out when I'm off base. Say what I need to hear. Guide me
to address what needs to happen to make this right, to see
God redeem this, to not let this define or control me.*

And that invitation is coupled with an openness to humbly receive the response—even if it's sometimes painful to
hear—because it embraces one more God-inspired proverb:
"Better is open rebuke than hidden love. Wounds from a
friend can be trusted."[11]

The Resulting Bond

Phrases like *blood brother* and *soulmate* are common in
modern vernacular. Not surprisingly, they invoke intimate
components of our humanness (blood and soul) to describe
a kind of cherished relationship that is valued and longed
for—universally sought though seldom found.

James follows his "confess your sins to each other" call
with a powerful statement about the effect such a bond can
have. He closes his epistle with these words: "My brothers
and sisters, if one of you should wander from the truth
and someone should bring that person back, remember
this: Whoever turns a sinner from the error of their way
will save them from death and cover over a multitude of
sins."[12] That soul-altering impact flows out of what Scripture describes as an agape connection,[13] a union unlike any
other. Unique. Distinct. Holy, even. It's a spiritual bond
forged by transparency, energized by intimacy, and sealed
by covenant. David and Jonathan experienced it when,
after confiding their hearts' true conditions with each
other, Scripture says "Jonathan became one in spirit with

11. Proverbs 27:5–6.   12. James 5:19–20.   13. See John 13:34 and 15:12. We'll
dive fully into this in chapter 6.

David,"[14] or literally, "the 'nephesh' of Jonathan became knit to the 'nephesh' of David." Their relationship entered a soul-based, God-anointed level—the kind Solomon later described as "a friend who sticks closer than a brother."[15]

The wonder of this bond is that it isn't dependent on how long or how well those entering it have known each other. While shared trial or crisis can accelerate it, the connection activates when one exposed heart is simply extended toward another and is responded to with an equally unguarded embrace. It can happen in literally any setting, between any Christ-indwelt people, sometimes without words even being spoken.

I was in attendance at a ministry conference where the speaker spontaneously invited anyone who felt their soul was aching and broken to make their way to the front where someone could meet them and speak blessing into their heart on God's behalf. Shortly thereafter a man quietly walked toward the front, and I noticed no one was stepping up to meet him. I was just a part of the crowd, but I guess the pastor in me felt some responsibility in such a moment, so I made my way toward him so he wouldn't be alone. As I approached him he looked at me with eyes full of silent desperation for God's touch, absolutely vulnerable, trusting whomever God would bring to meet his utterly exposed heart.

No words were exchanged. I found myself reaching out and tightly embracing him. He melted into my arms, and I closed my eyes, leaned toward his ear, and began praying blessing over him. In that moment, my own heart unlocked toward his. I was *with* him in our spirits, not knowing a single detail of his life or how to pray specifically about

14. 1 Samuel 18:1.　15. Proverbs 18:24.

what prompted him to expose his soul. But it didn't matter. I sensed God's Spirit breathing out from me, into his heart, and somehow returning to my own with its renewing power. We were bonded: nephesh to nephesh, open soul to open soul.

It was more than emotional or experiential; it was substantive. Visceral. Real. And it instilled a distinct, heaven-provided strength within each of us for what lay ahead.

This type of exchange doesn't require such a dramatic setting. It can happen in small or large doses, in private or public contexts, individually or in a group. When we humbly expose our truest selves to others, we open the channel through which ongoing doses of the gospel can be dispensed. Our burdens are revealed, fellow believers are given the opportunity to carry them, and "in this way [we] fulfill the law of Christ"[16]—which is to love each other on the deepest heart level.[17] We live out what Jesus prayed for his followers, for them to "be one, Father, just as you are in me and I am in you."[18]

Perhaps you've tasted it yourself. It's the essence of soul-level connection, and it's intended to be a normal, even daily, part of a life lived to the fullest.

———

Before we move on, an important note: the honest revelations and confessions we've discussed don't automatically guarantee the kinds of soul-bonding responses we hope for. Not everyone is ready to accept the unfiltered truth shared by a fully exposed heart nor are they equipped to respond in grace when it is. As a pastor I've actually had people stop

16. Galatians 6:2.   17. 1 Peter 1:22.   18. John 17:21.

attending our church because they heard me admit I still battle lust. I've watched friends distance themselves relationally because I confessed negative or superior attitudes I sometimes harbor toward others. Heck, I've lost others' respect just because they found out I don't like coffee.

But when I reflect on the people with whom I share the most meaningful and lasting friendships—those who care for me most deeply and value me most highly—they are almost without exception those I have invited to know my ugliest truths. My worst weaknesses. My most shameful moments. My most vulnerable secrets. They are the ones who know and hold my heart, who have stuck with me, and who have become my greatest source of strength. When you inventory your best and truest friends, perhaps you see a similar pattern.

Now imagine a community where this kind of dynamic is not only consistently pursued but genuinely experienced. Such an environment would stand out as radically distinct in a world of manufactured facades, conditional friendship, and wary guardedness. It would profoundly impact the emotional and spiritual health of those involved in it. It would mark its participants as those being transformed by Jesus.

This rare but remarkable brand of community is the next stop on our journey.

6

God's Ingenious Design for Authentic Community

Picture it: A typical, nondescript group of believers. People of varying ages and stations in life. Not a whole lot in common other than their love for Jesus.

But when they get together, something extraordinary happens.

They reveal their truest selves unreservedly to each other. They move toward one another's hearts in purposeful, spiritually charged support. Honesty, transparency, and understanding consistently mark their interactions. They share their secrets and keep each other's confidences. They band together in love to spur each other toward who they want to be. They earnestly pray for and with one another, applying God's Word effectively to each other's current situations. And they genuinely listen to each other—not just to what is being said but also to what lies beneath their spoken words.

They then respond to one another the way they believe Jesus would in that moment. They love being together, checking in often through the course of their weekly routines and walking away from their shared times cared for, strengthened, challenged, and energized.

Sound like a pipe dream? Perhaps. But if God can be taken at his word, not only is this kind of soul-connected community possible, it's intended to be normative among those who gather as the body of Christ.[a]

The phrase *foxhole buddies* is used to describe a deep camaraderie formed among soldiers who share hastily dug bunkers near a battle's front lines, spitting distance from enemy forces intent on killing them. Imminent threat creates implicit trust, shared vulnerability, and friendship forged in the fires of war. Many of these friendships last a lifetime, not merely because a collection of people wear the same country's uniform but because, in the face of fierce opposition, they make a conscious choice to entrust each other with their very lives.

God's design for spiritual community reflects a similar ethos. We're compatriots in a battleground every bit as real, serving a cause all the more important, forming a bond even greater in allegiance.

Sadly, however, that's not always the experience of Christian groups gathered in the real world. Sarah is an example. She walked away from involvement in her church's small group, admitting she hardly understood the reasons herself. The people were kind enough. The meetings devoted solid time to studying the Bible, sharing typical prayer requests, exchanging small talk, and catching up on family and work. The participants served together at a homeless shelter and even partnered to sponsor several children from developing countries. But when she'd say goodbye until the next week's gathering, she'd return home with a profound sense of loneliness. Something significant was missing, something her soul couldn't identify but that left her feeling empty and disconnected.

Sarah reflected that people in the group never really knew her, nor she them. They knew *about* her, but they didn't know the real her—the internal struggles she carried from her past, the self-doubt she wrestled with, the disappointments and unmet longings she couldn't seem to overcome. She didn't feel invited to reveal those parts of herself and seldom saw anyone else do so. On the rare occasions when someone did express something more difficult or personal, they were met with quick-fix advice, casual Scripture quotations, or an awkward silence and "thanks for sharing" comment before moving on to safer topics.

So she stopped attending. She decided what she was looking for was something the group wasn't able, or perhaps was never intended, to give. Maybe God should be enough to meet whatever need her heart was craving and her time was better spent coping with personal, private issues in personal, private ways.

Sarah's story parallels those of countless others in Bible-believing church settings who venture into Christian community with great expectations only to be left disappointed, still hungry for something they simply won't find.

What groups like Sarah's are missing—what her spirit instinctively longs for—is a fundamental, albeit scarcely encountered, component of God's design for authentic community. It's such a critical element, we would do well to camp here long enough to fully grasp what it is and how it's designed to work. And we'll learn that not only is it a provision Jesus considered a big enough deal to make the focal point of his final instructions before the cross but, as a feat of spiritual engineering, it's pure genius.

The Vertical "Pipeline"

It starts with Jesus's directive to his disciples (and to us) to establish a consistent, unblocked channel of heart-to-heart contact between his heart and their own—a spiritual pipeline of intentional, personal connection. He called this "abiding" in him.[1] It would serve as the active conduit through which his agape love would continuously flow into their individual souls,[2] the means by which his love would, as Paul would later say, be "poured out into our hearts through the Holy Spirit, who has been given to us."[3]

Much like a solar panel captures doses of the sun's radiating power, the intently submitted heart acts as a receptor cell capable of absorbing God's life-giving energy—his spiritually charged, perfect love. It then becomes enabled to dispense that charge toward others.

---

1. John 15:4–10 ESV. Much more about "abiding" will follow in chapter 9.
2. John 15:9.   3. Romans 5:5.

The Horizontal "Pipelines"

Jesus then introduced what he called a "new command"—for his followers to establish a second, active interconnection between their own hearts and the hearts of others. He charged them to "love one another."[4]

He'd already reaffirmed the "greatest commandment," which included the directive to channel God's agape love toward their neighbors (including their enemies).[5] But this command was "new" in that it called on them to establish a two-way pipeline with each other, through which they would, concurrently, *actively dispense* and *willingly receive* doses of the agape love they would absorb from him.[b]

A new operating system was thus established. Christ's followers were to open their individual hearts "vertically" to tap directly into God's flowing love ("abide in my love"), then mutually channel that love "horizontally" in a two-way current into one another's hearts ("love one another"), spiritually energizing each other simultaneously.

Reflect on the implications of this "new command" for us today. Some of us have become more than adept at pouring out love acts toward others through the first of the horizontal pipelines. We've taken seriously God's call to "love [our] neighbor," sacrificing ourselves to serve, draw out, listen to, and care for those in our ministry sphere. We can feel a measure of spiritual satisfaction, if not pride, in doing so. But we're capable of using that one-way focus to mask a reluctance, even an unwillingness, to open the second horizontal pipeline—the one that invites and allows others to pour out God's love toward us.

At first blush it seems noble. We're being selfless, others-focused, esteeming others better than ourselves. But it can very subtly serve as a self-protective deflection from admitting we also need to be *recipients*: willing to humbly expose our own weaknesses and receive care, support, and input. This can become especially true in longtime spiritual leaders and pastors.

Airline preflight safety instructions give parents a counterintuitive directive: in the event of sudden cabin pressure change, parents are told to put on their own oxygen mask before helping children with theirs. They're no good to anyone if they're depleted to the point of unconsciousness. The two-way channel established by the "new command" similarly provides the means by which Christ supplies his spiritual oxygen to everyone in his community of followers.

The "One Anothers"

This is where the "one anothers" of the New Testament come into play.

Jesus manifested God's nature—which the Bible says is agape love[6]—and displayed it tangibly through two complementary elements: "grace and truth."[7] Believers are instructed to do the same through the nearly sixty actions and attitudes given to live out with each other. Notice how the "one anothers" fall naturally into these same "grace and truth" groupings.

We're called to acts of *grace* (unprovoked, unearned favor and blessing; acceptance and intimacy; value and worth), such as to

- be devoted to one another[8]
- honor and accept one another[9]
- warmly greet one another[10]
- wash one another's feet[11]
- refrain from passing judgment or attacking one another[12]
- encourage, serve, and forgive each other[13]
- show one another patience and forbearance, equal concern, humility, kindness, and compassion[14]

We're also called to expressions of *truth* (accurate revelations of both one's own inmost condition and God's guidance for righteousness, wisdom, direction, and perspective), such as to

- dwell in God's Word with each other, teaching and admonishing one another[15]

6. 1 John 4:8, 16.   7. John 1:14, 17.   8. Romans 12:10.   9. Romans 15:7.
10. 1 Corinthians 16:20.   11. John 13:4–5.   12. Romans 14:13; Galatians 5:15.
13. 1 Thessalonians 5:11; Hebrews 3:13; Ephesians 4:32; Galatians 5:13.
14. Ephesians 4:2, 32; Colossians 3:13; 1 Corinthians 12:25; Philippians 2:3.
15. Colossians 3:16.

- sing God's Word to one another[16]
- confess sins to one another[17]
- tell one another the truth[18]
- instruct one another[19]
- spur each other toward love and good deeds[20]

Put them all together and they embody the overarching, most oft-repeated "one another"—love one another.

The Koinonia

This uniquely functioning dynamic, this Level 3 heart interconnection, was to become the cornerstone of the new community Jesus established for his followers until his return.

The New Testament actually gives it a formal name: *koinonia*, or "the fellowship." First designated as such just after the church's birth at Pentecost,[21] Scripture employs

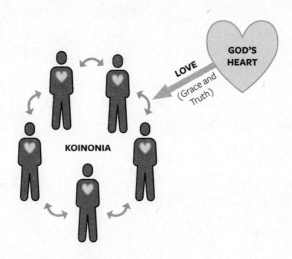

---

16. Ephesians 5:19.   17. James 5:16.   18. Colossians 3:9.   19. Romans 15:14.
20. Hebrews 10:24.   21. Acts 2:42 ESV.

the common word for "community," then earmarks a distinct, elevated type of it by adding the definite article, distinguishing it as not just ordinary "fellowship" but "*the* fellowship"—the extraordinary interaction of God-touched hearts gathering to funnel his love into one another's hearts.[c]

Enacting this special, soul-to-soul relationship would be so life-giving, Jesus said, that it would bring its participants a depth of joy he called "complete."[22] And its impact would be so noticeable to a watching world, simply observing it in action would serve as an undeniable identifier of Jesus-touched people. "By this," he said, "everyone will know that you are my disciples."[23]

This is Level 3 community. This is what your heart is meant to experience.

I recall one of the first times I experienced it for myself. I was attending a typical Bible study—the only kind I'd known. A dozen or so people were sitting in a living room with Bibles open, summarizing the correct interpretation of a biblical text and articulating general life application principles. I gave what I thought was a particularly astute answer to one of the discussion questions when Stephanie quietly interjected from across the circle.

"Tom, if it's okay, can I tell you something I think Jesus might want you to hear right now?"

"Um, sure," I said a bit uneasily. This was new. And a little weird.

She held my gaze and spoke directly to me in a gentle, caring voice. "I think he'd want you to know that you don't have to prove yourself anymore."

22. John 15:11.   23. John 13:35.

I sensed an immediate urge to push back, though I didn't quite know what I'd be pushing against. But her words were so kind and tender, my defenses were disarmed.

She continued, "I just wonder sometimes if you feel like you've always got to be at the top of your game. Like if you don't work harder than everybody else, you might be seen as a slacker. Like the minute you screw up, people will reject you and you'll lose their respect."

It felt like she had snuck into my house and read my journal, except I didn't keep one. I wondered how she could possibly know all this about me without my having exposed it.

"That can put an incredible amount of pressure on a person," she said. "They can never relax. They've always got to keep going, keep producing, keep meeting everyone's expectations. It can be exhausting."

It was as if she'd taken a scalpel and ever so carefully sliced through the tough exterior of my projecting image to expose my heart. But instead of criticizing the deficiencies it revealed, she poured a balm of love and acceptance over it.

"You need to know that you're amazing," she said. "You've been shaped and formed by Jesus, and we all just want you to know that we respect you like crazy. We're in your corner forever. And we're proud of you."

My eyes welled with tears. It caught me by surprise, overwhelmed me, touched me in a way I hadn't ever experienced in a group setting. And I wasn't even quite sure what "it" was. But I knew I wanted more of it.

"It" was a dose of heart-level community. Koinonia.

When fully functioning, our interconnecting hearts become tangible dispensers of God's love. We become his hands and feet, his arms and legs, his ears and voice. The gospel's power flows through our veins as we move toward each other in penetrative, spiritual impact.

People sometimes use the expression that believers can be "Jesus with skin on." But Jesus already has skin. He doesn't need body doubles. We're more than representatives of Jesus's body; we're multipliers of his heart. We extend his presence, love, and influence exponentially into each other's souls in his name.

Don't look now but this dynamic isn't intended to be a specialized task performed by select Christ followers. It's not an optional program. It's a central practice of what God meant by "church"—the primary means by which he pours his love into a group that he says forms "one body," where "each member belongs to all the others."[24]

Romans 12 drips with Paul's call to koinonia. He begins by mentioning the spiritual gifts given to Jesus followers, designed to be activated toward each other in the body of Christ as they consider each other more important than themselves.[25] Then, beginning in verse 9, he offers a litany of imperatives to live out qualities reflecting God's love and character. It's sometimes lost in the English translation, but every one of the directives in Romans 12:9–21 is presented in the second-person plural, intended to be performed as a group in the context of community.

Think about what that would look like when we paraphrase the list and turn the imperatives into descriptions of a group actually doing it:

They don't just pretend that they love others. They really love them. They hate what is wrong. They stand together on the side of the good. They love each other with genuine affection, and

24. Romans 12:5.   25. Romans 12:3–8.

they take delight in honoring each other. They're never lazy in their work, but they join forces to serve the Lord enthusiastically.

They express gladness together for all God is planning for them. They stand united in patience during trouble, and they're always prayerful together. When God's children are in need, they team up to help them out. And they are in the habit of inviting guests home for dinner or, if they need lodging, for the night.

If people persecute them because they're Christians, they don't curse them; they pray together that God will bless them. When others are happy, they're happy with them. If they are sad, they share their sorrow. They live in harmony with each other. They don't try to act important, but they enjoy the company of ordinary people. And they don't think their group knows it all!

They never pay back evil for evil to anyone. They do things together in such a way that everyone can see they are honorable. They do their part to live in peace with everyone, as much as possible.

As dear friends, they never avenge themselves. They leave that to God. For they know and remind each other what is written: "I will take vengeance; I will repay those who deserve it, says the Lord."

Instead, together they do what the Scriptures say: if their enemies are hungry, they team up to feed them. If they are thirsty, they unite to give them something to drink, and their enemies are ashamed of what they've done to them. They don't let evil get the best of them, but together they conquer evil by doing good.[26]

Read that description again, and this time, picture the faces of people in the groups you have been, or are currently,

26. Author's paraphrase of Romans 12:9–21 NLT.

involved with. Pause after each statement to ask yourself these questions:

- When was the last time you were in an environment where you actually, literally, observed this particular act happening?
- Can this statement be accurately made today about your group?
- What gets in the way of this practice occurring in your own circle of relationships?
- What would happen if you initiated this act in your current group or friendship circle?
- Do you currently have an environment where this aspect of spiritual community could be introduced?

If you aren't satisfied with your answers, the good news is that a set of practical catalysts for fully functioning koinonia—which we'll look at next—can go a long way toward making the picture a reality.

7

How to Make Soul-Connected Community Happen

Some of the most unsafe places on earth can at times be found inside the walls of churches and home groups. Cliché, pretense, shame, and judgment make the honest unwelcome and the welcomed dishonest. Intense pressure to keep up appearances or preserve personal comfort pushes the door to heart-level community closed. Or slams it shut.

It can be different. Radically, beautifully different. Genuine koinonia can wash the stink off our unsavory experiences with pseudo-fellowship and replace it with life-giving soul connectivity. It happens when we eliminate koinonia's inhibitors[a] and proactively implement four critical catalysts that help establish heart-level, authentic spiritual community.

Intentionality

Pigcasso, a two-year-old pig from Cape Town, South Africa, became an international sensation when someone stuck an artist's brush in her mouth and she began randomly slathering paint on a canvas. Her handiwork captured the public's fancy, and several of her paintings subsequently sold for more than $5,000 each.[b]

Not to you or me, of course. That would be stupid. With all due respect to the artistic swine of the world, we understand that true masterpieces don't just happen; they're skillfully and purposefully crafted.

The same can be said of heart-level community. It isn't produced by shoving the paintbrush of small group programming into the mouths of saints gathered in the same room. It must be deliberately enacted and consciously sustained.

The apostles baked the language of intentionality into their instructions for the church's interactions. "Love one another deeply," Peter instructed gathered believers, "from the heart."[1] In a different epistle, Paul wrote, "The goal of this command is love, which comes from a pure heart and a good conscience and a sincere faith."[2] Unless someone directly steers a collection of people in the direction of Level 3 interaction, human nature defaults to operating on a need-to-know basis, with almost no one ever qualifying as needing to know.

In my young believer days I attended midweek prayer meetings where brothers and sisters in Christ gathered to, presumably, care for one another by taking each other's weightiest needs before God's throne. When the invitation was given to share matters for prayer, a handful of typical

1. 1 Peter 1:22; see also 4:8.   2. 1 Timothy 1:5.

requests would be made. The country's leaders. Protection for the troops. Great Aunt Gertrude's bunions. Someone would always make sure to remind everyone to pray for the peace of Jerusalem.

And then the most common prayer request would be shared. The pastor would ask if there were any "unspoken requests." Hands would shoot up all over the auditorium. While some of these matters may have been left unnamed for legitimate reasons, I knew firsthand that many were kept secret out of fear and relational self-protection.

On one occasion a family friend lifted her hand and said, "Pastor, I have an unspoken *praise*."

Good grief.

Can you find any scriptural precedent for someone asking others to approach God on their behalf without divulging what it is they're approaching him about? If I trust you enough to ask your help carrying my burden before the Father in heaven, shouldn't I trust you enough to let you know what that burden is?

When someone decides to take the lead toward a better way, significant change can follow.

Tyler was just such a change agent. As a small group leader, he had grown tired of the charade. Attendance was always spotty, people would give safe, pat answers, and no one ever ventured below the surface of each other's lives. After their group's annual tradition of taking the summer months off—which was another thing that bugged him (if community is the lifeblood of spiritual health, how do you just suspend it for a quarter of the year?)—he decided it was time to do something about it. He led off the first meeting with a firm but sincere statement:

Let me tell you why I'm here. It's to be part of something God designed and that my heart needs—a place where I can be completely honest and open about what I'm going through and others can too. Where we invite Jesus to meet us and speak through each other from his Word to move us through the tough stuff together to become more like him. So for me, this is a "no BS" zone. I need you to know the true me. I'm going to invite you to see me as I am and move toward me courageously as Jesus's rep in my life, as I do the same with you. I'm asking you to do that with me.

The group lost some people after that. Long-timers, in fact. They decided it wasn't what they'd signed up for. But most of the group welcomed the new direction and made a commitment to follow it through.

It revolutionized their experience. Together they began to taste the authentic intimacy and substantive personal growth they knew they craved but didn't know how to find. It wasn't perfect, but it was fundamentally different. The group was transformed.

Tyler has since said he feels it's essential to make sure the group's purpose is restated every time they meet—sometimes by him, sometimes (even better) by others—in order to constantly refresh their commitment and help newcomers understand what they're about. When they do, it works.

Initiation

Someone has to go first.

Every now and then you'll hear a story about some formal poolside party—a wedding reception or gala—where everyone winds up jumping fully clothed into the pool in laughter and frivolity. It usually involves copious amounts of alcohol, but it also makes for a lifelong memory. In order for that memory to happen, though, someone has to be the first to jump into the pool with his tuxedo on and see whether others will follow. If they do, it's a party. If they don't, the guy in the pool is just an idiot who won't get his rental deposit back.

When it comes to creating an environment where people push through their self-protective barriers and expose their true heart's condition to each other, someone has to be the first to jump in the pool—to step into the waters of vulnerability and take the very real chance they'll be left alone in that position, intensifying the ache they're exposing if others don't follow. It's a genuine risk. But for Level 3 honest community to happen, it's a risk someone must take.

The question is, Are you willing to be that someone?

A group of Christian friends had gathered to watch a football game together and were hanging out afterward, shooting the breeze before heading home. As they chatted, someone casually asked Seth how his new job was going. "Good. Yeah, it's good," he responded. A couple others began chiming in about their own work. Then Seth suddenly spoke up again. "No, wait," he said. "I didn't tell you guys the truth. I got let go last week."

Things instantly got quiet. He proceeded to say he'd not only been fired but had been accused of misconduct. He paused, then added soberly, "And it's true." There was an awkward silence, followed by a misplaced attempt at humor. But then others started offering genuine care and sympathy. One man spoke up about how he'd been reported to HR recently. Another confessed he'd once been "terminated for cause," but to save face had always told people he'd been laid off due to budget cuts. The group asked Seth caring but important questions, offered encouragement and support, and asked if he needed financial help. They circled up and prayed over him.

Koinonia had broken out. Seth had chosen to reveal his truest self when no one else was doing so. He'd jumped into the pool.

Jesus modeled this in the garden of Gethsemane. Agonizing over the sacrifice he was about to make on the cross, he entrusted his heart to his companions and invited them to enter his moment of raw anguish. "My soul is overwhelmed with sorrow to the point of death," he said. "Stay here and keep watch with me."[3]

His disciples failed to join him in those troubled waters, falling asleep rather than offering him soul-to-soul support when he needed it most. Even as they flunked their first test to live out the new command he had issued only hours before, Jesus continued modeling it for them by honestly expressing his disappointment at their response—but from a heart still exposed and ready to receive their love.[4]

Paul later reflected the same practice when he wrote, "We have spoken freely to you, Corinthians, and opened wide our hearts to you. We are not withholding our affection from you, but you are withholding yours from us. As a fair exchange—I speak as to my children—open wide your hearts also."[5]

Sometimes all it takes is a sincere invitation. My wife and I were heading to our small group meeting one cold winter evening when we got into one of those knockdown, drag-out arguments that always seem to happen when you're on the

3. Matthew 26:38.   4. Matthew 26:40–41.   5. 2 Corinthians 6:11–13.

way to church stuff. We pulled into the host home's drive-
way and just sat there in the dark, seething in our anger and
preparing to turn around and head home.

Another couple in the group, Dave and Karen, walked past
us on their way into the meeting. But just before entering the
house, Karen turned, looked in our direction, strode back,
and stood in front of our car. All we saw was her silhouette
as she called out, "Are you guys fighting?"

We didn't answer. And she didn't wait for one. "Well,
come on in and let's deal with it together," she said. Our
every impulse was to avoid exposing the embarrassing state
of our marriage at that moment. But Karen's invitation told
us, "This is exactly what this group is for. It's a place where
your genuine condition can be safely welcomed, seen, and
processed with others in love." We made our way into the
meeting, and everyone jumped into the pool with us to wade
through our mess together. We were saturated with a healing
dose of Level 3 community.

Someone needs to initiate the pool-jumping. When they
do, everyone else can respond to the invitation to follow
them into the water.

Mutuality

One of the Protestant Reformation's most profound rediscover-
ies came to be called the priesthood of all believers, which main-
tains that regardless of someone's history, position, knowledge
level, or accomplishment, *any* carrier of God's Spirit can not
only approach him directly and without hesitation but also
carry out ministry to others equally and effectively.[6]

6. 1 Peter 2:4–9; Hebrews 4:14–16; 1 Timothy 2:5; Romans 12:1–8.

Do we still believe that? If every member of Christ's body is gifted and empowered by the Spirit now residing within their soul, even a new believer can challenge, encourage, and counsel longtime disciples in their faith. No pedigree or qualifiers are required. They hold equal privilege—and responsibility—to channel God's grace and truth to others in his name.

Level 3 community puts the priesthood of all believers into motion. It is thus always mutually active, never passive. No one is a spectator. Spiritual gifts aren't just enacted by paid professionals; they're equally employed by everyone, including those who may initially need help recognizing they possess any.

Jennifer is one of them. An introverted, stay-at-home mom, she attended her life group consistently but quietly. She seldom spoke up, partially because of her personality and partially because when she did have something to add, others who tended to talk too quickly and too much jumped in before she got up her courage. One evening, someone in the group interrupted one of the quick-talkers and, seemingly out of nowhere, said, "Hang on a second. Jennifer, you look like you're thinking something. I'd really like to hear what's going through your mind as you're hearing this."

What came out of Jennifer in the next few moments was nothing short of anointed. Her words exuded wisdom and insight. People began to recognize that Jennifer had something to say. Or, rather, that God had something to say through her—something every bit as valuable as what came from the louder, more educated, or more experienced members of the gathering.

Because koinonia is designed to be a dual-pipeline inter-connection—both receiving and dispensing doses of God's love—it should never become a setting where one person assumes the mantle of resident guru, imparting their superior knowledge to notetakers who sit at their feet. It's a place where everyone listens, prays for wisdom, accesses God's Word, and actively moves toward their brothers and sisters to make spiritual impact.

Sports fans love their superstars. But sometimes, when the superstar goes down with an injury, fans are shocked to see the team go on a winning streak. Journeyman players start coming through in the clutch; role players begin producing like all-stars. Without the luxury of depending on their MVP to work his or her magic, the club finds it can play better working as a team than waiting for one headliner to carry them to victory.

I've seen it happen countless times in the body of Christ. Those who previously hid behind the excuse of "I don't know the Bible well enough to say anything" or "I wouldn't know how to help" take a prayerful step of faith toward a fellow believer in Christ's name, not even knowing what they'll say or do as they initiate it. And God shows up.

I've watched as a reserved woman spontaneously sang a worship song directly to a hulking man across the circle—shocked at herself for doing it—and saw him dissolve into tears as God spoke to him through her gesture.[c] I've seen one friend ask another a simple follow-up question that drew out a much deeper matter hiding behind his initial words, leading to confession of a long-neglected issue he needed to see God address in his life. On multiple occasions I've witnessed someone read a Bible passage that just "happened" to pop into their mind as someone else shared the challenges they were facing. I've gotten chills observing someone stand up unprompted, walk across the room, and embrace another who had disclosed a devastatingly painful part of their personal journey, weeping together as others followed suit and gathered around them in support and prayer. I've seen sins confessed and forgiven, money collected and shared, and encouragement injected like medicine into the soul.

The wonder of koinonia is unlocked when those joining in community understand and practice united mutuality in the way they tangibly love one another.

Consistency

Hebrews 10:25 sure gets a bad rap.

The oft-quoted lines, "[Let us not give] up meeting together, as some are in the habit of doing," have regularly been used to beat people up about missing Sunday services or not signing up to work in the nursery. Shame, it seems, is still a powerful motivator.

But the writer of Hebrews didn't pen those words to keep butts in seats. He was addressing a very real need in the human heart. The human soul doesn't soften and open and then remain in that condition indefinitely. It naturally retracts, recloses, and hardens. The letter to the Hebrews waves a flag to make sure we recognize the single most important provision God has given to prevent that from happening: consistent, repeated infusions of heart-penetrating encouragement from fellow believers.

Hebrews 10 urges Christ followers toward sustained involvement in active koinonia for the sake of their fellow believers as much as for themselves. To "spur one another on toward love."[7] Earlier in the same letter, the writer makes a similar but even stronger statement: "See to it, brothers and sisters, that none of you has a sinful, unbelieving heart that turns away from the living God. But encourage one another daily, as long as it is called 'Today,' so that none of you may be hardened by sin's deceitfulness."[8] Consistent activation of soul-connected community isn't an issue of mandated obedience; it's a matter of spiritual life and death.

I've been learning, training, and living out these principles for over forty years. But here's the Level 3 honest, right-here-and-now truth from my own life: It doesn't matter how long I've been at it; the moment I let active, soul-to-soul community slip from my regular rhythm (and I occasionally do), heart-hardening effects begin to set in. And I mean immediately. They can be imperceptible at first, but the crust begins to form. My spirit drifts toward cynicism. Pride and selfishness creep into my mind. I naturally begin to isolate and self-excuse. It's like weight training or distance running. The positive effects that took months, even years, of hard work to build up can atrophy in mere days of inactivity.

What's worse, when my regularity wanes I'm even more prone to cover up that fact than I was before I became the guy who studies and teaches all this. Because I'm now someone who "should know better." I would surely never let it happen in my own life.

I don't need consistent koinonia in my life because the Bible requires it; I need it because my heart is desperate for it—and desperate without it. The smallest interruption alters my soul's condition and course and can lead me to darker places than I could ever imagine I'd go.

7. Hebrews 10:24.   8. Hebrews 3:12–13.

Like the constant, mini corrections we make while steering to keep our car on the road, consistent, repeated, even daily contact in heart-level community is key to avoiding spiritual drift. Many ministries offer life groups, cell groups, home groups, or various support groups as one of a smorgasbord of available spiritual growth options for their attendees. But if koinonia isn't intended to be just an elective but the foundation for full spiritual health, it must become more than an if-I-can-fit-it-into-my-schedule program.

The Outcome

No one is suggesting these catalysts for heart-transparent community are easy to implement. Enacting them is one of the most challenging and demanding practices a group of believers can choose to pursue. That's one of the reasons it's so rare. But those who consistently do so almost universally report that the payoff is worth the labor.

Listen to Ephesians 4's profound summary of the fruit produced by courageous, heart-honest community. As we inject doses of love's grace and truth into each other's open hearts, "the body of Christ may be built up until we all reach unity in the faith and in the knowledge of the Son of God and become mature, attaining to the whole measure of the fullness of Christ."[9]

Reflect on those words again. Unity. Knowledge. Maturity. The *whole measure of the fullness of Christ.* They're experienced by a group that creates heart-to-heart connection, channeling it all toward each other.

That's a goal worth going hard after, one you'll never regret pursuing.

9. Ephesians 4:12–13.

8

Soft Heart, Firm Boundaries

An axiom of life: *Any truly good idea will eventually be monetized, weaponized, or both.*

Living from a fully opened, fully authentic heart is a good idea. And as such, it has been exploited for nefarious purposes. When I speak on this topic, it's not uncommon for someone to approach me afterward with a heartbreaking story of being cruelly betrayed with information they shared in a presumably trusted environment. Others recount experiencing deep wounds sustained when someone plunged the knife of anger and condemnation in the name of "just being honest." Some object to the notion of open-hearted living altogether, arguing that unrestricted self-revelation is reckless and irresponsible, inviting needless and sometimes irreversible damage.

They make a valid point. Many of us know the anguish of revealing private information only to have it used against us in devastating fashion. Secrets are carelessly outed without permission or regard. A litigious culture makes any admission of wrongdoing vulnerable to legal action. "The truth hurts," the saying goes, but sometimes it destroys.

That's why it's important to recognize the complementary principles Scripture includes in its call to an open heart. It has never been God's intention, or his practice, to demand indiscriminate exposure of everything true about us to everyone we encounter.

The Bible incorporates provisions for establishing wise boundaries to guard against the destructive misuse of genuine vulnerability. If an intruder breaks into your home, a commitment to Level 3 honesty holds you under no obligation to inform the perp where you hide your valuables or what room your kids are huddled in. Savvy coexists with authenticity.

The challenge we face is that those qualities tend to be viewed as mutually exclusive. Either we're soft-hearted, open, and exposed, or we're street-smart, restrictive, and harsh. The alternative God advocates is that of being fully soul-genuine while simultaneously exercising the courage to maintain firm boundaries against abuse and exploitation.[a]

How do those seemingly antithetical practices harmonize? The answer lies in implementing some basic, sound counsel from God's Word.

The Principles of Discretion and Propriety

Ecclesiastes 3's brilliant poem speaks of an appropriate time for "every activity under the heavens," including "a time to be silent and a time to speak."[1] A commitment to heart-level

1. Ecclesiastes 3:1, 7.

honesty doesn't mean everyone in our world is granted equal access to what is true within us, nor does it mean we express everything we think and feel to everyone we meet. The time, setting, audience, and potential impact inform our actions, which are guided by love and edification. Freedom is tempered with wisdom. Details are governed by propriety.

Paul instructed us to "speak truthfully to your neighbor," but "only what is helpful for building others up according to their needs, that it may benefit those who listen."[2] Romans 14:19 calls it "mutual edification." We are free in our self-revelation, but our freedom should express itself only in ways that draw both those to whom we express it and ourselves closer to holiness and purity.

In practical terms, this means that if you're married, you don't confess emotional or physical attraction to your co-worker in the name of transparency. Doing so doesn't draw them or you toward righteousness; it only makes "provision for the flesh."[3] It doesn't mean you should point out every imperfection you notice in someone's work in the name of being truthful. If the invitation to offer critique hasn't been given, doing so doesn't build them up, it demoralizes them. It means you don't share the privacy of what happens in your bedroom with the general public. Doing so serves no constructive purpose.

All of this is driven by the installation of Bible-sourced "wisdom" into our open-souled expressions. Wisdom enables us to consider our audience, gauge and purify our motives, and exercise prudence in our interactions. Notice how discretion and wisdom are consistently paired in the book of Proverbs:

2. Ephesians 4:25, 29.   3. Romans 13:14 KJV.

- "Discretion will protect you, and understanding will guard you. Wisdom will save you from the ways of wicked men, from men whose words are perverse."[4]
- "My son, pay attention to my wisdom, turn your ear to my words of insight, that you may maintain discretion and your lips may preserve knowledge."[5]
- "I, wisdom, dwell together with prudence; I possess knowledge and discretion."[6]

We could summarize all that advice in one, overarching statement: when it comes to self-disclosure don't be dumb.

Wisdom serves as both guide and guard, steering our freed hearts toward appropriate interactions where discretion and propriety build up others and avoid destructive impact. As the fifteenth-century philosopher Voltaire is often quoted as saying, "Everything you say should be true, but not everything true should be said."

The Principle of Discernment

The sad reality is that our world is full of unsafe and untrustworthy people. And while God has made it clear that we're not to judge others by pronouncing condemnation or enacting punishment, we're also instructed to discern those who abuse and misuse what is entrusted to them and then adjust our interactions with them accordingly.

"Do not give dogs what is sacred," Jesus said. "Do not throw your pearls to pigs. If you do, they may trample them under their feet, and turn and tear you to pieces."[7] None of us wants to make a habit of labeling people as dogs or pigs (at

4. Proverbs 2:11–12.   5. Proverbs 5:1–2.   6. Proverbs 8:12.   7. Matthew 7:6.

least not when we're at our best), but Christ's words indicate we'll encounter people he describes as such, who display an inability to handle what's been given to them with maturity. And he warns his followers to discern who they are and erect boundaries to prevent their abuse.

The Bible uses two descriptors in particular for those with whom we need to exercise such discernment: the weak and the fool. The weak includes those who show themselves unable to handle vulnerable truth in healthy ways; their own choices and journeys are negatively affected by witnessing our candor. "Be careful," Paul writes, "that the exercise of your rights does not become a stumbling block to the weak."[8] He goes on to urge restraint in practicing our freedoms— what could be called "establishing a boundary"—when we are around those who are weak, to guard against enabling them toward sin as a result.[9]

The fool includes those who exhibit consistent patterns of exploiting others for self-serving purposes or who abuse others' expressions of genuineness. We are instructed never to pronounce someone a fool,[10] but we're likewise charged with the task of discerning those around us who exhibit the qualities of one and maintaining healthy guardrails in our exchanges with them.

Proverbs notably lists opposite actions toward a fool in consecutive verses: "Do not answer a fool according to his folly, or you yourself will be just like him. Answer a fool according to his folly, or he will be wise in his own eyes."[11] The statements aren't contradictory; they're dual instructions indicating the importance of discerning distinct times

8. 1 Corinthians 8:9.   9. 1 Corinthians 8:13.   10. Matthew 5:22.
11. Proverbs 26:4–5.

when unguarded interaction with a foolish person may be appropriate and other times when it would not.

Do you know someone who exhibits these traits? Sometimes the most soft-hearted, loving act you can express toward them is to recognize their condition and maintain a healthy boundary to mitigate the damage they might do to themselves or others with shared vulnerabilities. We can display a humble and truthful heart toward our world while establishing a perimeter that exercises restraint among those not yet ready to properly handle it.

The Law of Love

Jeremy is a self-described "straight shooter." He prides himself in saying exactly what he thinks and feels at all times, being brutally honest about both his past experiences and his present opinions. I've seen him tell people he's just met that they could stand to drop a few pounds. He has shared uncomfortably intimate details of his sexual experiences and fantasies in casual settings. He's been known to offer unsolicited critique and advice to complete strangers on everything from their fashion choices to their voting habits to the way they smell. He considers it a compliment when people refer to him as having no filter. He says he's "just keeping it real" and "telling it like it is."

Jeremy's shock-and-awe approach serves an unhealthy, self-centered purpose. His commitment to explicit self-expression isn't motivated by love. It represents a misguided attempt to establish an identity at the expense of others and an illegitimate effort to make an impact in his world.

Undergirding everything we do with the full freedom God gives our hearts lies one supreme law: the law of love. Our souls aren't set free to serve self or indulge our freedoms for our own benefit. We're to be guided by the new nature embedded within us: God's agape love—the covenantal decision to give sacrificially what is best for others without demand for anything in return.

"You, my brothers and sisters, were called to be free," Paul wrote. "But do not use your freedom to indulge the flesh; rather, serve one another humbly in love."[12] For the fully freed heart, every honest expression may be "lawful," but that doesn't make it "helpful."[13] The commitment to heart-level honesty doesn't give us license to word-vomit our opinions or bazooka-blast people with our frankness. All the Bible's principles for gracious speech still apply:

- "always full of grace" and "seasoned with salt"[14]
- free from anything "unwholesome"[15]
- kind, like honey that is "sweet to the soul and healing to the bones"[16]

Regardless of how honest and forthright our interactions may be, a "gentle answer"—the kind Proverbs says turns away wrath[17]—is the order of the day, every day. Even when we find it necessary to speak hard truth or defend orthodoxy against culture's gravitational pull, we convey it gently and respectfully, in love.[18] When we confront others boldly, we do it seeking their good and restoration.[19] When we express anger toward another, we do so cleansed of sin.[20]

And when we're wounded or betrayed, when our most natural impulse is to harden our hearts toward the offender

---

12. Galatians 5:13.   13. 1 Corinthians 6:12 NKJV.   14. Colossians 4:6.
15. Ephesians 4:29.   16. Proverbs 16:24.   17. Proverbs 15:1.
18. Ephesians 4:15.   19. Galatians 6:1.   20. Ephesians 4:25–26.

to protect ourselves from ever being hurt by them again, God calls us to keep our hearts soft even while we enact legitimate boundaries. We do it not out of vindictiveness or vengeance but out of compassion and love.[21] We treat them as fellow recipients of God's undeserved mercy and grace, with the hope they will someday be transformed by the same God-drenched deliverance that has set our own hearts free.

The Exercise of Faith

Even when soft-hearted yet firm boundaries are in place, the risk always exists for flawed humans to fail each other. When we choose to present an unshielded heart to our world, we can count on being disappointed, rejected, or worse. Never underestimate the human capacity for cruelty.

Every time we experience injury at the hands of another, we're tested again. We'll wonder whether it's worth the cost to continue exposing our truest selves to others when they so often respond by inflicting harm on us. Do we turn our boundaries into impenetrable walls, or do we continue seeking healthy environments where we can drop our guard, knowing we're making ourselves susceptible to the same injury again and again?

This is where what we say is true of God as our protector and provider becomes more than sentimental rhetoric. Rather than turn a calloused heart toward those who disappoint us, God invites us to consistently bring our damaged souls back to him for restoration and healing. Our Father is the advocate of the heart-wounded,[22] the comforter of the soul-afflicted,[23] the healer of the spirit-crushed.[24] Disappointment and pain create opportunities to draw near to the

21. Romans 12:17–18.   22. Psalm 18:2; Isaiah 61:1.
23. Psalms 94:19; 119:50, 76.   24. Psalms 34:18; 147:3.

One who promises never to allow our injuries to become permanent or fatal.

The human body is equipped with a wondrous, built-in provision whereby it automatically shifts into repair mode as it enters the deeper stages of sleep. At least a dozen therapeutic functions initiate naturally the moment deep sleep begins. God offers our souls an even more profound provision. When we bring an injured spirit directly to his compassionate touch, he commences a spiritual healing process that penetrates to the very core of our deepest selves.

Take full advantage of that provision. Allow your heart to hear and embrace the promise of Psalm 34: "The LORD is close to the brokenhearted; he rescues those whose spirits are crushed. The righteous person faces many troubles, but the LORD comes to the rescue each time. For the LORD protects the bones of the righteous; not one of them is broken!"[25] We entrust ourselves to God's restorative touch so that we can keep our hearts intact, softened and opened toward our world and offered freely again despite the continued risk.

A word here to those who have suffered abuse—who offered an unguarded, vulnerable heart and watched someone use that privileged position to wound you bodily, emotionally, or spiritually. The damage inflicted was devastating and debilitating. Perhaps no one knows how deeply those wounds penetrated or how severely they affect you to this day.

Please hear this. God knows. He grieves over it. And he will never diminish the significance of your experience by asking you to quickly "move on" or to expose yourself to the risk of repeating the abuse. He has included the pursuit of justice and the protection of the violated among his

25. Psalm 34:18–20 NLT.

boundaries for guarding the soul's care for just that reason. Preventing an abuser from being given the opportunity to repeat their abuse is part of his call to defend the weakened, victimized, and mistreated.[26] As that boundary stands guard over your heart to prohibit further abuse, know that the Father in heaven weeps with you over your current pain. He recognizes what you're carrying. He enters into it and remains beside you through it. When Hagar sat despairing over the abuse she had endured, the God of heaven came to her, gaining the name El Roi, "the God who sees me."[27] He saw Hagar. He sees you.

His words in Psalm 147 are especially for you: "He heals the brokenhearted and binds up their wounds."[28] He wants to heal your broken heart from the inside. That doesn't mean asking you to return to the risk of suffering again at the hands of your abuser. Rather, it means bestowing wholeness and healing that will bring your heart, scarred but restored, to a place where it can feel the security and strength to once again present itself to others, to connect on the level of deepest trust, joy, and love.

When these principles and provisions are combined in one heart, they allow us to live out one of Jesus's most vivid images describing healthy spiritual living in a fallen world. He told his followers, "I am sending you out like sheep among wolves. Therefore be as shrewd as snakes and as innocent as doves."[29]

Read that entire Matthew 10 passage through the lens of a life dedicated to coupling a soft heart with firm boundaries,

26. Proverbs 31:8–9.   27. Genesis 16:13.   28. Psalm 147:3.   29. Matthew 10:16.

and you'll see both clearly represented in Jesus's instructions. He directs his disciples to move into their world giving liberally, offering themselves gently and peaceably, and extending their hearts as instruments through which the Spirit will speak. In the same breath he warns them to beware of those who destroy the vulnerable. To be on guard against those who betray and sell others out. To create distance between themselves and those who persecute and abuse. He presumes both can happen simultaneously as they live from a redeemed, trusting spirit.

Our widely opened hearts carry the capacity to be street-smart, wise, and aware. We can exercise shrewd discernment to recognize potential abuse and interact in ways that guard against exploitation. At the same time we can remain vulnerable and trusting, gentle as sheep and innocent as doves, allowing ourselves to know and be fully known. To communicate and care from our truest, most authentic selves.

That combination is so winsome that when the watching world encounters such a heart, it can't help but conclude it is witnessing the mark of God's otherworldly stamp on a human soul.

9

What Happens When You Get Soul-Honest with Jesus

This one seems like a no-brainer.

Of course our souls are fully open to God. He already sees everything within us, all the time. We don't need to do anything to make that happen; it's inherent to his God-ness. Besides, doesn't the Bible say he knows when we sit and rise, perceives our thoughts from afar, and is familiar with all our ways?[1] We can assume our connection with God is the most natural, effortless facet of living from an unhidden heart.

But that would be a mistake. It's precisely because he's so close that our relational depth with Jesus can be so easily neglected.

Most of the walls in my house are decorated with pictures or paintings. At least, I think they are. I couldn't for the life

1. Psalm 139:2–3.

of me tell you what picture is on what wall. They've hung in the same spots for so long, they've become invisible. I walk past them every day, but they meld into the background to the point where I seldom notice them anymore. All I know for sure is that I've never dusted any of them.

Something similar can happen with our most familiar relationships. They become such a fixed part of the land-scape, we stop giving them the same attention we pay to our newer ones. Whether it's our spouses, relatives, or oldest friends, our closest relationships often become our laziest.

With God, this familiar laziness can sneak up on us even more subtly. We know he's always there, but since we don't typically see him physically or hear him audibly, in-the-moment awareness of his presence can fade like pictures on the walls.

Jesus calls us to something different.

In his final conversation with his disciples, perhaps pointing toward roadside vineyards as they walked toward Gethsemane, he said this:

Abide in Me, and I in you. As the branch cannot bear fruit of itself, unless it abides in the vine, neither can you, unless you abide in Me.

"I am the vine, you *are* the branches. He who abides in Me, and I in him, bears much fruit; for without Me you can do nothing." . . .

As the Father loved Me, I also have loved you; abide in My love. If you keep My commandments, you will abide in My love, just as I have kept My Father's commandments and abide in His love.[2]

2. John 15:4–5, 9–10 NKJV.

116

The Greek for abide in that statement (*meno*) doesn't have a perfect English equivalent, and that's unfortunate. It's been translated a number of ways,[a] but no translation quite captures its full meaning. It specifically points to the active, integrative junction between grapevine and branch—the unobstructed flow of nutrients that subsequently produces fruit. Ed Hellman, horticulturist at Oregon State University, explains it this way: "Water and dissolved mineral nutrients absorbed by the roots are moved upward in the xylem to all parts of the grapevine. The phloem is the conduit primarily for food materials and their derivatives to be moved throughout the plant."[b] I'm no expert, but it doesn't take a rocket scientist to understand that if the xylem thingy isn't connecting to the phloem thingy, the nutrient thingies don't get through, and the grape thingies stop growing.

Jesus invoked this vine-and-branch imagery to convey something profoundly essential to our relationship with him. The means we've been given to absorb spiritual nutrients from him—the way we obtain what we most need to grow in him—is to "abide" in him, *to consciously join our hearts to his own heart*.[c] It's an intentional, personal engagement—my fully open heart *being* with Jesus. An intimate, active, flowing connection.

That sounds easy. Even appealing. But in truth, my own journey to embrace it has proved to be a difficult one. My early spiritual formation was built on a foundation of obedience, not intimacy. Spiritual vibrancy, so I thought, came by checking off a series of boxes: spiritual disciplines, serving, giving, resisting temptation, doing right. I viewed direct contact with Jesus a lot like visiting my grandmother or going to the dentist—good and important responsibilities to keep but mostly done out of obligation and to appease my conscience. Obedience was the important thing. As the old hymn said, "Trust and *obey*, for there's no other way to be happy in Jesus."

My path was interrupted by a spiritual director who gently pointed out that, yes, Jesus included obedience in his definition of abiding, but the commands he most emphasized obeying were themselves acts of heart-to-heart connection.[3] My spiritual mentor then followed up that observation with a question that rocked me: "Do you even *want* personal intimacy with Jesus?"

I had to admit I wasn't sure. Pursuing intimacy with Christ as a real, present person requires spiritual awareness and emotional investment. It isn't "measurable" in the same way performance-based obedience is. It's *being*, not doing.

But the more I considered it, the more I decided I at least *wanted* to want it. And it set me on a course that continues to this day: to shift my internal values, to lay aside the "duty mentality" and remind myself again and again that intimately connecting with Jesus is enough to give me worth . . . and simultaneously fulfill my highest duty.

Opening the Vine-to-Branch Connection

So how does it happen? How do we establish this vine-to-branch connection and ensure it stays open and flowing? As with everything we've explored, it has to do with opening a fully honest heart. Consider three tangible components we can intentionally build into our contact with the Savior, presenting a soul open to "abide" in his vine.

3. John 15:10–12; 2 John 5–6.

1. Intentional Focus

Making heart-to-heart contact with Jesus starts with activating our awareness of his here-and-now, personal presence.

Any time my wife and I go to a restaurant with sports playing on mounted televisions, she purposefully chooses a table to position me so I can't see any screens. She knows I'm utterly incapable of focusing on her if there's any sporting activity in my line of sight, regardless of what the sport may be. I'll quickly zone out, lost in some high school field hockey tournament in South Dakota. At that moment I may be with her, but I'm not *with* her. Her love language is focused attention. She wants me to look her in the eye, to be "all there" with her. When I'm not but try to pretend I am, things can get ugly.

Most of us know the feeling of being physically present with someone who is checked out, bodily in the room but personally disengaged. Abiding requires making deliberate contact between our heart and God's in real time—recognizing his nearness and making ourselves cognizant of his presence. Spiritually looking Jesus in the eye.

Psalm 46:10 speaks of being "still" in God's presence,[d] a condition a later psalm likens to a quieted, "weaned child with its mother."[4] In a frenzied world where every waking minute is bombarded with sound and light waves demanding attention, the act of "slowing"—eliminating distraction and inclining our hearts to our very present God—won't happen without conscious choice.

We could call this creating an "abiding moment." It need not be long or drawn out. It can be prompted deliberately, the way a smartwatch can be set to alert us when it's time to stand up and walk around. Brother Lawrence, the seventeenth-century

4. Psalm 131:2.

Carmelite lay monk, built such an exercise into his renowned collection, *The Practice of the Presence of God with Spiritual Maxims*. He wrote:

> A little lifting up of the heart suffices; a little remembrance of God, an interior act of adoration, even though made on the march and with sword in hand, are prayers which, short though they may be, are nevertheless very pleasing to God, and far from making a soldier lose his courage on the most dangerous occasions, bolster it. Let him then think of God as much as possible so that he will gradually become accustomed to this little but holy exercise; no one will notice it and nothing is easier than to repeat often during the day these little acts of interior adoration.[e]

This isn't just a spiritual discipline; it's the master valve controlling the channel through which all subsequent spiritual disciplines (prayer, Scripture study, meditation, worship, etc.) flow. It's the essence of James's invitation, "Come near to God and he will come near to you."[5] Bring your whole self before Christ. When you're there, be "all there."

Take a beat before we go on and ask yourself how regularly this occurs in your current, daily practice. Is your soul in conscious contact with the Savior's heart of love at this moment? If you pause after reading this paragraph to overtly make yourself aware of God's presence in the room with you right now, linger in that awareness.

2. Passive Positioning

Our physical bodies synthesize vitamin D while doing nothing more than exposing our skin to the sun's rays. Often

5. James 4:8.

the first treatment doctors recommend for seasonal affective disorder is, if at all possible, to just get some sun. Similarly, once we've established conscious awareness of God's heart, the abiding process involves what we might call *passive positioning*, where we assume the dependent, internal posture of a recipient. We simply place ourselves before him, knowing that, like being in the sun, nothing more is necessary for our souls to soak in his nourishment.

The familiar biblical account of Mary and Martha illustrates this vividly. Martha was dutifully serving her Savior, but Mary chose to sit at his feet, listening and learning. Jesus commended Mary for choosing "what is better"—the action he said was the "only one" necessary at that moment.[6]

Those of us with multitasking, type-A personalities tend to struggle with this. We get restless quickly. There's a whole lot of waiting here, a whole lot of (seemingly) "nothing" going on. But if we stay long enough for the fog to clear, God uses our passive receptivity to clear out the clutter, unclog the blockages, and refill our spiritual tanks with his overflowing supply of love and grace.

Those who exercise passive positioning sometimes report feeling a surprising wave of tenderness wash over them. Affection toward God. Closeness to him. If that happens, we shouldn't be afraid of it or dismiss it as sentimentality. We're encountering the endearment Paul described when he called God our "Abba." *Papa.* Allow yourself to see God's warm countenance, to feel his personal embrace. It's what he repeatedly expresses as his own greatest desire toward us: his arms enfolding us, his presence calming us, his acceptance and grace enveloping us.[7]

6. Luke 10:41–42.   7 Matthew 11:28–30; 23:37.

121

Again, pause here for a moment and reflect on how recently or how often you enact this practice within your soul. Read through Psalm 46 slowly and carefully and notice what Scripture says this heart-level, receptive posture toward God's heart does. Then create some space to initiate it, unhurriedly and expectantly, and enjoy the effect it produces within you.

3. Active Absorption

Viticulturists tell us the grapevine's branches don't just receive nutrients from the trunk, they actively *draw* them, like a nursing child draws milk from their mother. Jesus invites us to do the same. "Abide in me," he said, *"and I will abide in you."*[8] We can proactively draw spiritual nutrients from Christ's loving supply. He generates spiritual nourishment for us; we move further toward him and ask for more.

Scripture records what many consider a curious story reflecting this kind of exchange. Jacob encountered God's manifested physical presence outside his encampment late one night. Recognizing an opportunity, he tenaciously held on to God, seeking his blessing, wrestling with him through the night, not relenting until he received it.[9]

Some wild speculation exists over God's purpose behind this long scuffle. The Almighty could have easily taken Jake out in the first round but instead allowed the match to continue through the night, finally dislocating his "opponent's" hip after hours of struggle.

Theories on this encounter abound, but one thing appears certain: Jacob desperately wanted something from God—more of what he knew only God could give him—and was willing to hold him as tightly as he could, all night

8. John 15:4 ISV, italics added.   9. Genesis 32:24–30.

if necessary, in order to get it. God seems to give us permission to pursue him for greater doses of spiritual vitality and blessing, to pester him for more of himself.

There's a beautiful ridgeline trail near our home where you can see the mountains in one direction and the ocean in the other. At times I'll walk it and picture God's throne above the whole scene, the majesty of what's below pointing toward his transcendent glory above. I'll physically lift my hands and reach heavenward as I walk, drinking in the presence of the One who reigns over everything I see, including myself. "I don't even know what I'm trying to draw from you right now," I'll say, "but I'll take whatever you're willing to give. Just give me more of *you*."

The Lord has said, "You will seek me and find me when you seek me with all your heart."[10] Brother Lawrence put it this way: "Think often on God, by day, by night, in your business and even in your diversions. He is always near you and with you; leave him not alone."[f]

Make this an intentional, active practice between Christ's heart and your own. Ask him for more of himself. Draw more life from the vine. Don't leave him alone.

The "Abide in Me" Payoff

When a heart makes this kind of sustained connection with God's heart of love—when it learns to "abide" in him with a fully opened soul—something profound happens. The connection unlocks a level of intimate honesty with God that most have never experienced . . . and might not even think is permissible. Those who enact it find they can be utterly

10. Jeremiah 29:13.

themselves around God without fear of reprisal. They can expose their truest, even ugliest side, free from shame or condemnation. They see God as a companion they can confide in, a friend they can vent to. They approach him, as Paul described, "with freedom and confidence."[11]

Perhaps no one in Scripture epitomizes this Level 3 honesty with God more than David, whose ways of expressing himself are so raw and unfiltered, some find them disturbing. He dances undignified before the Lord. He makes audacious requests of him. He grouses to him about his situation, his disappointments, and his discouragements. He even lashes out at him in anger and frustration. He sounds accusatory at times, pressing God about where he's hiding or why, if he's as good as he claims, he hasn't answered or intervened.[12]

And then there are the imprecatory psalms, where David calls on God to break people's teeth, blind them, and cause their utter ruin and death.[g] That seems a bit harsh.

But it's clear he is angry and frustrated, weary of everyone bailing out, letting him down, and making his life harder. So he asks to speak with the manager. He's invited into a safe space where he can vent, open the release valve, and let the black smoke of disappointment billow out. It diffuses into the clean air of God's sovereign grace, and he catches his breath. The outpoured gunk is replaced by a cleansing assurance and wholeness. He regains his perspective and moves on. Until the next time.

———

Behind this entire heart-to-heart "abiding" thing—and the gut-level honesty with God it produces—stands one,

11. Ephesians 3:12.   12. Psalm 13:1–2.

preeminent purpose. Above everything else, what Christ wants through all of it is for us to *know* him.[13] Intimately. Personally. Tenderly. From our truest, inmost selves.[14]

And *knowing* God is entirely different than knowing *about* God.

As a kid I idolized Derrel "Bud" Harrelson, who played shortstop for the New York Mets. I knew everything a fan could know about him: born in Fremont, California, he played sixteen seasons in the major leagues and was a gold glover and two-time all-star. To this day I can recite most of his career stats from memory. I emulated his footwork on the field, wore his same uniform number 3 on my high school team, and attempted to become a switch hitter to be more like him. I even met him once—behind the dugout before a game in Pittsburgh—and he signed a ball for me that sits prominently on my shelf, along with autographed bats and pictures of him that hang on my office walls. I really, really know Bud Harrelson.

But I don't. I don't *know* Bud Harrelson, and he never knew me. We never once went to lunch together. I was never invited to his home and never caught a movie with him. If I'd showed up at his house unannounced or persistently tried to reach him by phone, I'd have probably been reported as a stalker. He never thought of me or learned my name, and I don't hold any intimate knowledge of his personal life, feelings, or perspectives. I don't actually *know* Bud Harrelson at all.

God wants us to know him. Really know him. And that's what living from a fully opened soul with Jesus allows us to do. We're not just studying him, talking about him, or

13. Philippians 3:8, 10.   14. Jeremiah 9:24.

serving him. We're abiding dynamically in him, interacting freely with him, experiencing life alongside him—because we're actually connected *to* him. Person to person. Spirit to spirit. Heart to heart.

Choosing to live from an open soul produces many benefits, but this one is—and always will be—the highest and greatest.

10

Facilitating Heart-Open Koinonia

Lightning rods don't generate electricity. They simply attract, receive, and conduct the energy of lightning when it strikes. When that happens, it makes for some spectacular pictures.

God's transformative power produces a charge not unlike the presence of electricity in the atmosphere, with groups of heart-connected believers serving as lightning rods that attract, receive, and conduct its charge. The gatherings don't generate the current; they simply serve as instruments to invite and channel it.

It's no surprise, then, that the Bible doesn't offer a prescription for *producing* the energizing power of koinonia. Instead, those who desire to experience it learn to focus on creating an environment structured to anticipate and optimize the effect of God's life-giving love as it's received.

Formal small groups aren't the only place where this soul-bonded community can happen. It can be experienced formally or informally, one-on-one or in groups of varying sizes, in Bible studies, support groups, family units, or just in circles of friends who desire to connect on an authentic, honest heart level.

What follows are suggestions for helping a group move toward it, drawing on scriptural principles to offer practical guidelines for any gathering of people desiring full-hearted koinonia.

1. Establish a clear picture of koinonia as the purpose and goal

People gather in groups for widely varying reasons, with even wider expectations. The vision for pursuing soul-level relationship under Christ needs consistent restatement, perhaps every time the group meets. Overtly remind the participants why they're there with an invitation to unite in the pursuit of that dynamic.

This can be accomplished by introducing the gathering time with a brief but clear reiteration of its purpose. Summarize the meaning of "heart-open community" by reading a portion of Scripture that highlights it (such as Acts 2:42–47 or Romans 12:4–21), or simply explaining it in your own words. Here are a couple sample statements:

Sample 1
There are probably any number of gatherings of friends going on around town tonight. There are Bible studies, support groups, meetings in bars, sports leagues, craft clubs, game nights, and people just hanging together.

So what makes this group different? There is a dynamic God created that we are meant to experience, one that can make what happens here completely distinct from any other gathering. It happens because the Holy Spirit resides in the hearts of each member of the body of Christ.

When the "carriers" of God's Spirit assemble—when they do so in Christ's name and then actively open their hearts toward him and one another—something happens. The Spirit of God moves in their midst. He pours out his heart on them. He does something that extends beyond their intellect or emotions. He touches their souls and energizes them spiritually.

That's what we're here to pursue together tonight. It doesn't happen just because we've shown up and are Christ followers. It happens if we intentionally open our hearts toward him and toward each other in his name.

Sample 2

We live in a world where we seldom experience something we were designed for. It's called soul-level community.

"Community" as the Bible describes it means being in open-hearted connection with God and others. And it's why we get together like this. It means we have a place where our true selves can be revealed and accepted:

- *where there's no fear of shame for our inadequacies*
- *where we can admit our sins and failures and find help and forgiveness*
- *where we can be injected with courage to walk in obedience to God's direction for our lives*

It doesn't happen in our daily routine because it's not "natural" in a fallen world. But God made us for it, and he wants us to experience it with him. So tonight we're here to pursue that level of community. It'll happen if we invite Christ to be in our midst, to stir us, and to move through us to channel his heart and love to one another.

2. Invite the participants to present their hearts fully to God

Provide an opportunity at the start of the gathering for everyone to personally and individually approach God heart-to-heart and to engage intimately with their Creator. Read pertinent Scripture and prompt them to give themselves to God, invite his presence to impact their lives, and offer themselves to listen to him and serve as his mouthpiece, arms, hands, and heart to others in the group. If someone is adept at leading worship music, consider including that element. Here are a couple sample statements:

Sample 1

Let me invite you right now to take a moment to present yourself to God as his agent to touch someone else in our group. I know you're probably tired. Or you might be really hurting, and it's not natural to go into a group looking to meet others' needs when you've got plenty of your own.

But when you do, Christ's Spirit springs into action inside you. He will move in you and through you; he will empower you as you present yourself to him. The Bible says God supplies the energy to do his work when we submit ourselves for that purpose.[1] Are you willing to do that with him?

I want to suggest you turn to the Father in your heart and say, "Right now I present myself to you, surrendered for you to use me to be your ears, your mouth, and your hands toward others in your family tonight."

Sample 2

Before we start connecting with each other today, let's take a moment to focus on and connect with our Creator. We're going to spend time opening up to each other, confiding in

---

1. Philippians 2:13; Colossians 1:29.

each other, and encouraging each other, but if that's going to have any effect other than on a natural, earthly level, we've got to first be connected to God, to be filled by him so that the effect can be spiritual and supernatural.

So let's start by approaching him. And as we do, let's consciously present our time, our spiritual gifts, and ourselves to him afresh. Let's invite him to be active here, to give us spiritual insight into each other's lives, and to speak to us and through us and through his Word tonight.

3. Invite the participants to reveal their hearts and lives to each other

Give everyone an opportunity to talk about their personal lives, situations, joys, and challenges.[a]

A significant means of helping one another expose the heart's true condition is through the method modeled so well by Jesus—the art of effective question-asking. The facilitator can set the tone by introducing a pertinent question or offering a list of questions from which individuals can choose to respond. But everyone in the group can and should also be shepherded to learn how to ask pertinent and heart-inviting questions of one another.

The best questions are open-ended (cannot be answered merely yes or no), individualized so that they can only be answered by the person they are directed toward, and crafted to invite internal rather than external reflections from the respondent's life. Below are samples of the type of prompts that invite the group to expose their true selves to one another.

Sample 1 (statements to complete)

In a moment, we're going to invite everyone to open our lives and hearts to each other and to God. As we do, there's a list of various phrases we might use—ones that go hard after real, life-changing interaction with each other and with God. So think about how you might finish one of these statements tonight:

- The current condition of my heart is _____ .
- The biggest blockage between God and me right now is _____ .
- One specific action I need to take to obey God is _____ .
- What God has been convicting me about lately is _____ .
- A struggle I'm dealing with right now is _____ .
- A way I blew it big-time this week is _____ .
- Something I'm frustrated with right now is _____ .
- Something I'm grappling with right now is _____ .
- What's really going on in my thought life right now is _____ .
- A situation I want to invite your insights about is _____ .
- A temptation I'm really battling right now is _____ .
- Something I need help with is _____ .

The facilitator might also choose one or two primer questions to throw out to the group, such as those in the sample below, encouraging the participants to ask each other follow-up questions to the answers given.

Sample 2 (questions to answer)
- What is the current state of your soul?

- What one thing has most consumed your emotional energies lately?

- Is your spiritual tank filling, draining, or plateauing right now, and why?

- What has given you joy recently?

- What is the most significant thing you've experienced since our last conversation?

- What do you really need prayer for right now?

- How are you really doing right now?

- How has your relationship with God been lately?

- What temptation(s) are you struggling with right now?

- What prayer have you seen God answer, or not yet answer, lately?

The Proverbs 20:5 principle comes into play here: "The purposes of a person's heart are deep waters, but one who has insight draws them out." The human heart's truest condition and motives often need to be "drawn out" by others who care about them. This can be done by encouraging the group to engage in two key practices of heart-level koinonia.

Listening beneath another's words. People often bury the lead when they answer direct questions. When group members are tuned in to the Holy Spirit, they can sometimes hear something mentioned casually that warrants a follow-up question. Perhaps the person glosses over an important point or their body language indicates discomfort about something they're not saying. The courage to respond to the Spirit's prompts in that moment can open the door for the person to allow their brothers and sisters into the area of life they most need God's truth and grace to address.

"Pursuing" each other. The rule of thumb when someone answers a question is to do something noticeably contrary to human nature: resist the urge to respond with advice or one's own story, and *ask another question.*[b] This practice of "pursuing" recognizes that people almost never start with the core issue; they mention externals and peripherals but need someone to, again, draw their hearts out further. If group members find it challenging to know what follow-up questions to ask in the moment (a common occurrence), the go-to statement can simply be, "Say more about that." Most people will, if invited.

Our culture operates under the unwritten rule of responding to the question, "How are you doing?" with the innocuous one-word answer, "Fine." If you immediately follow that response by looking the person in the eye and asking, "I mean, how are you *really* doing?" you may find they understand you are genuinely inviting them to reveal a truer condition of their circumstances and heart.

4. Prompt those present to move toward one another's opened hearts with grace and truth

Remember, it isn't merely the exposure of a soul that produces transformation. It's bringing that exposed soul into contact with God's life-producing change agents. His primary instruments in that regard are his Word, his indwelling Spirit, and the grace and truth injections dispensed through fellow believers.

This is where koinonia becomes a very active, participatory dynamic. Help the group think proactively about how they can approach the needs and opportunities exposed by others with the use of their own spiritual gifts and the enactment of the "one anothers" right then and there in the gathering. Encourage them to be in constant, silent prayer as the time together progresses, asking the Holy Spirit to give insight into ways they can respond to what they're observing and hearing.

Below are sample statements that can be used to prompt active, participatory movement toward one another during a meeting.

Samples

- If Christ were in the room right now, say what you think he would express to the person who just shared.
- If God brings a Scripture to mind that applies to what you hear, look it up and share it.
- If you sense something unsettling in your spirit about how someone is responding to a circumstance in their life, or if you have a hunch about what might be at the core of their situation, ask if you can share it, then do so graciously and honestly.
- If you feel it would be appropriate to stop in the middle of the meeting and pray together for a situation, or over someone who shares a need, speak up to suggest it and take the lead to do it.
- If you sense an impulse to embrace or physically comfort someone (of the same gender) in an emotional or vulnerable moment, get up and do so if they are amenable to it.
- If you feel someone needs correction or challenge about something you sense could be unhealthy thinking or perspective, ask their permission to offer it from an attitude of love and support.
- If you possess the resources to meet a physical, financial, or material need through a tangible action, offer to do so.

- If you have no idea what to say or do in response, pray quietly where you are and ask God to give you direction, then act or speak, trusting God to give you the words to say.[c]

When people hold back or don't engage with others during this time, it creates an important moment to process it as a group to ask what is holding them back. Prod them a bit to initiate. Raise their awareness of the responsibility and privilege to become agents of God's love in that moment, even (and especially) when they aren't quite sure of themselves in doing so.

The goal is for the group to step into each other's lives both graciously and courageously. Not in an attempt to solve everyone's problems or to give quick answers and token advice but to walk with them through what they're facing in their real, heart-level lives. This is the essence of koinonia, "loving each other from the heart," in action.

5. Steer formal Scripture study components toward heart-open, Level 3 honest interaction and application

A group gathered for the purpose of koinonia can still include times of concentrated, even formal, Bible study. Some groups utilize preselected curriculum or follow a Sunday sermon–based, follow-up discussion plan as part of their meetings.

Whether a group uses a "start with life and apply the Bible" approach (as Jesus most often did) or a "start with the Bible and apply it to life" approach (e.g., book studies, curriculums), avoid making Bible study portions of group meetings a talking-head instructional time or knowledge-driven study. Focus instead on crafting increasingly open-ended, self-reflective questions that move the discussion toward open-hearted, honest application of God's Word.

Notice how the sample questions below move progressively from Level 1, content-focused Bible interaction ("What does the passage say?"), to Level 2, principle-focused Bible interaction ("What does the passage mean?"), to Level 3, application-focused Bible interaction ("How does it apply to me and/or people I touch, especially in the present?").

Level 1 (content-focused) Bible Interaction Sample Questions
- What is happening in this passage? When is it happening? Who is involved? What is the context?
- What is the original intent of this passage? What would the original audience have been hearing and understanding about this?
- What truth about God, people, and/or life on earth does this portion of Scripture reveal or address?

Level 2 (principle-focused) Bible Interaction Sample Questions
- Why did God include this in his book?
- What transferrable principle(s) about life is it illustrating or teaching?
- Where does this principle show up in our current day?

Level 3 (application-focused) Bible Interaction Sample Questions
- In what situation or relationship does the truth or instruction conveyed in this passage show up in your life today?
- To what degree would you say you're implementing, or not implementing, this principle or practice in your current situations and choices? If you're not, what is holding you back?

- What do you need to do about it? How are you going to think, feel, choose, or act differently to reflect this truth in your current situation?

Don't get bogged down in intellectual/educational minutiae or theological wrangling in the group context (if such deeper study is needed, suggest or even assign it to be done outside the group time). Rather, focus on the same principles of honest, teachable interaction and mutual pursuit among the participants that they are already experiencing, as they apply God's truth to their lives and situations. Invite and allow God to minister—from his Word, through the group, to each other's hearts.

6. Eliminate koinonia killers

Both human nature and the enemy's wiles can sabotage heart-level community. A number of blocks to full koinonia often crop up in group settings—some consciously chosen, others unconsciously displayed. Below are samples of some of the most common. Watch for these, address them when you see them, and encourage those present to commit themselves to not allowing them to detract from the heart-level community the group is pursuing together.

Samples
- Misplaced humor: using sarcasm, jokes, or other attempts at humor to pull the tone away from deeper interaction and back toward the surface, masking or diverting from true issues[2]

2. Ephesians 5:4; Proverbs 14:13.

- Quick-fixes and clichés: attempting to solve someone's problem with profundities rather than entering into their shared situation and pain[3]

- Confessing others' sins: naming names and focusing on what others have done to wrong someone or oneself, rather than concentrating on and taking responsibility for one's own actions[4]

- Pooling our ignorance: drawing on human wisdom and advice rather than looking to Scripture as the source of truth and bringing the Bible to bear on the aspects of life being discussed[5]

- Harshness and impatience: pressuring or shaming rather than displaying gracious patience about others' progress or responsiveness[6]

- Bible academia: spouting Scripture quotations and facts as the definitive, final word in a display of intellectual prowess rather than processing their real-world, personal application[7]

- Dominating: overtalking rather than drawing on the entire group for sharing and responding; consistently turning the focus onto oneself rather than onto others[8]

- Passivity and isolation: attending without participating; remaining quiet rather than moving actively toward others[9]

- Hit-and-miss involvement: displaying a willingness to preempt regular attendance rather than prioritizing the group's gatherings and interactions[10]

3. Ephesians 5:6; 2 Timothy 2:14–16.   4. Proverbs 11:13; 20:19; James 5:16.
5. 1 Corinthians 1:28–31; 2:6–16.   6. 1 Thessalonians 5:14; 2 Thessalonians
3:14–15; Romans 14:1; 15:7.   7. 1 Corinthians 8:1–3; 2 Timothy 3:7.
8. Proverbs 10:19; 17:28; Philippians 2:3–4; James 1:19.   9. 2 Corinthians
6:11–13; 1 Peter 1:22; James 4:17.   10. Hebrews 10:23–25.

- Meeting-time-only community: limiting contact and interpersonal interaction to the set meeting times rather than involving others in the regular routines and communications of life (see "Encourage between-meeting contact")

7. Encourage between-meeting contact

While consistent gathering times serve as the cornerstone of functional, heart-level community, most of what Scripture describes as its activity requires consistent contact *outside* the confines of a group meeting. Biblical community extends to the routines of life, where the participants' relational circles expand to involve each other in daily practices. Serving one another, caring for each other, carrying one another's burdens—all require consistent touch points beyond a standing meeting. Urge your group to live out Scripture's "one anothers" and to exercise their spiritual gifts as a lifestyle, making koinonia a reflection of family rather than a function of program.

There is a wonder to God's provision of koinonia. It unites, heals, strengthens, and purifies. It creates a supernatural bond of love and belonging that can't be replicated anywhere else on earth. It is God's astounding mechanism for channeling his fullest joy, peace, and life to his people, through his people.

And while we can't produce it ourselves, we can position ourselves to receive it together, forming a soul-open, soul-honest connection that widens the pathway to receive its power.

Then, when the lightning does strike, we're ready.

Conclusion

After everything we've discussed in these pages—all the examining of God's design for the soul, all the calls to honesty and vulnerability, all the challenges to create environments of genuine soul-connection with our Savior and others—we come back to where we began, to the foundational question posed in the introduction, which I believe God asks each of us: Will you open your heart?

No one's forcing you. Not even Jesus. But he offers the invitation knowing that if you choose to move courageously, to present who you really are to yourself and to those around you, to take the risks that produce genuine community, to not just obey and serve the Lord but commune with him in intimate, soul-centered contact and companionship, you'll quickly begin to notice effects that are real, healthy, and life-changing.

Perhaps as you've walked through these pages, you've begun to see them already:

- You're finding yourself more fully present in your interactions—self-aware in the best sense of the word. You're more conscious of who you are and who you're not, and you're more comfortable in your own skin.

You notice you're freer in your self-expressions: what you feel, how you think, what you value and believe.

- You're becoming increasingly authentic and genuine with people. No one has to wonder what you're really thinking or not saying. You no longer feel like you're being held hostage by what you've done, where you've been, or the choices you've made. You're not masking how you're really doing or hiding your true emotions. You're more willingly revealing your truest self, even the raw and unpolished parts, without being controlled by guilt or regret.

- You're making sincere, intimate bonds among friends with whom a rich history is forming on a shared journey. You're connecting in vulnerable and significant relationships as part of a community functioning consistently on a foundation of full disclosure, mutual understanding and acceptance, and complete support and trust.

- You're regularly self-examining your motives and more readily inviting others to check them as well. You're less resistant to hearing even painful feedback because you have an increasing sense of being held tightly and accepted absolutely through any warranted or unwarranted criticism you may receive.

- You're praying more naturally. You're worshiping more meaningfully. You're discovering God's presence to be calming and peace-giving. You're enjoying simply being with him.

- You find yourself dreaming more boldly and longing more deeply, and you're feeling the freedom to share those dreams and longings in ways you wouldn't have before.

All of these effects arise naturally as a heart finds its freedom in full openness and authenticity. And as it happens within you, you'll notice one more thing: you'll genuinely like it. It's compelling and contagious—not just to others but within yourself. It's "life to the fullest"—exhilarating because it's what you were designed for. As you experience it, you'll more and more quickly recognize environments where it doesn't happen, and you'll be less and less satisfied in them. You'll crave this level of honesty, this atmosphere of belonging, this grace and acceptance. You'll find you don't want to be without it.

Think of it this way. You can spend a lifetime eating pastries from the local supermarket and be completely content, never the wiser. But should you ever find yourself in New York City's Little Italy, just once stop by the Caffé Palermo—affectionately known as the Cannoli King—and order a specialty cannoli fresh from their bakery. Then close your eyes and take a bite. From the moment you taste the delicate, flaky shell and to-die-for creamy filling, you'll never, ever be satisfied with a store-bought pastry again. You'll also have a whole new understanding of the classic line from *The Godfather*: "Leave the gun; take the cannoli."[a]

When we experience the heart-level honesty and community God designed us for, it's almost impossible to go back to life without it. We'll seek it out and do whatever it takes to ensure it stays a part of our daily rhythms and relationships because we know it's what allows us to live the way we were intended to—wholly alive and deeply loved as open-hearted, soul-connected people.

APPENDIX

A Word to Leaders and Pastors

If you're a ministry leader, you're a rare breed. You work long and hard to serve others for the cause of Christ. You inspire and organize. You teach, care, and pray. You model the Savior's ways, spread his truth, and reflect his grace. You don't do it for recognition, but even so, you aren't thanked nearly enough.

Along the way you may have become aware of something else that can be true of spiritual leaders, something far more prevalent than most realize: you can be deeply involved in— and committed to—helping people open their hearts and connect with God and others from their truest selves yet not actually do so yourself.

It's very common for those who point others toward soul-level honesty and community to operate from something less than it themselves. The demands of ministry—all the kingdom advancement and burden bearing and spiritual equipping and focusing on others' needs—can bring leaders to a place where they decide exposing their own soul's condition, especially its weakness, weariness, or woundedness, isn't necessary. Or important. Or even allowed.

It can happen subtly, even imperceptibly. And it may be difficult to admit. But take a moment to reflect honestly on some questions that can help you recognize whether it may have become true for you:

- How often do you publicly reveal current doubts, disappointments, or personal challenges to those you lead?

- Are your stories and references to temptation and sin in your life generally past rather than current examples?

- When you *do* speak of your own struggles, do you typically couple them with instruction on the correct biblical response to make it a teaching moment?

- Do you engage in worship differently in your own church or ministry setting than you do when you're simply an anonymous attender of a worship event elsewhere?

- When you prepare to teach, do you focus your energies on how to articulate God's truth for maximum effect in your hearers' lives and not so much on how to apply it to your own?

- Are you involved in a small group that you don't lead? If you do have such an outlet, does your awareness of your role as a spiritual leader influence how careful and calculated you are in your participation?

- How many people in your ministry scope have you specifically invited to ask you personal questions about your marriage and family relationships, your sexual purity, your attitudes toward people and the world, or the current condition of your soul? How many ever take you up on the offer?
- Do the people you lead ever see you weep?

If you as a leader find you aren't revealing the true state of your heart the same way you ask those you shepherd to reveal theirs, you have plenty of company—and some seemingly good reasons to back up your choice. For starters, you operate with a different level of responsibility than those you lead. Because of your position, the fallout could be far greater for you than for others if someone were to betray your trust and reveal something you've shared privately.

You're also their chief encourager and motivator. They look to you for inspiration, and if they sense doubt or discouragement in you, it could erode their confidence in the ministry's vision. You wouldn't get on a plane if the pilot confided he was unsure he could fly it. How could those you lead be expected to follow someone who's not completely convinced they know what they're doing, where they're going, or whether they're ever going to get there? Your influence could be significantly diminished if they see frailties they aren't equipped or mature enough to handle.

What's more, those you lead have their own struggles and loads to carry. It's logical to think there's no reason to burden them further with yours. It doesn't do them any favors if you distract them from dealing with their issues to concentrate on yours. People don't go to their doctor to hear her talk about her ailments; she's there to help patients treat their own.

And besides, people generally aren't looking for a broken leader anyway. They desire, even demand, that their shepherds have achieved a level of spiritual maturity and accomplishment that represents the pinnacle they themselves aspire to. Their sports heroes are world-class athletes; they expect their spiritual heroes to have world-class souls. They want to believe their leaders operate on a different playing field. Their motives are always pure and holy, they never argue with their spouses or lose their temper with their coworkers. And their poop doesn't smell.

Christian culture is likewise titillated by the notion that our pastors and spiritual leaders can be special. Anointed. Reaching heights that can put our ministry on the map. Far too many churches privately *want* a narcissist as their pastor. They're enthralled by the take-charge, "follow me and I'll lead you to the promised land" commander who marshals an army and charges the hill, making a name for their church and themselves in the process. They want a king like the other nations.[a]

That may be what the people you lead want, but it's not what they *need*. They need what the Bible consistently puts forward as its prescribed model: leaders who exemplify true, heart-level honesty—before God, within themselves, and among those they shepherd. When your people look at their leader, they need to see someone who lives what they call out in others: admission that they're a hot mess full of contradictions and inconsistencies, scarred and bruised and exposed, driven continually back to the soul-restoring heart of Christ.

Please hear this. God's call on those who lead in his name has always been first and foremost to be someone whose spirit is broken, whose heart is exposed, whose soul is connecting deeply and honestly with him first and with those they are leading next.

Is yours?

When those being shepherded have that in their leader, they relax in the knowledge they're following someone who understands and can relate to their situation, whose authentic self they know they're receiving. They see a fellow follower being embraced with the same grace-soaked acceptance they themselves are being offered. The people you lead need that in you. You need it in yourself.

You can move purposefully in that direction, and it can begin now.

Renew Direct Contact

It starts with reestablishing a free-flowing, unblocked conduit directly between your inmost heart and your Savior's. Jesus gave his followers the incredible provision discussed in chapter 9: "abiding" in him—the deliberate joining of your heart with Christ's is accomplished by intentionally lifting your spirit to him and placing it in direct contact with his. When was the last time you did that? Enact it. Again. Absorb his presence. Present your soul to his Spirit's revitalizing touch. You can do that now, in this moment, as you're reading this line.

Then picture God's Son walking alongside you, participating with you as you serve him in your ministry—whether it's meeting people, teaching, guiding, planning and organizing, or performing the menial tasks every leader sometimes needs to do as part of kingdom work. It's the difference between—as author and speaker Skye Jethani described it—doing ministry over God, under God, from God, or even *for* God, and doing it *with* God.[b]

My wife has routinely repeated the same mantra to me through my years of ministry: "The one thing your church needs most from their pastor is to know he has just been with Jesus." It's always had the curious effect of simultaneously relieving and convicting me. Mostly the latter. It reminds me (and I constantly need to be reminded) that it's always all about Jesus. Not my skills, not my vision, not my leadership. My humbled, vanquished, abiding-in-Jesus heart.

Reestablishing that God-aware, heart-to-heart channel will never become so routine and easy that it doesn't need consistent, intentional discipline. Everything else we do as ministry leaders hinges on this foundation. Jesus was serious when he said that unless that connection is open, we "can do nothing."[1]

Remove the Veneers

Next, we need to address the veneers we form over our hearts.

Almost every spiritual leader has them. They become so much a part of us, we can be oblivious to their presence. But they're there, thin layers of protection installed between ourselves and others, just clear enough to allow glimpses of our authentic selves but opaque enough to obscure what we don't want seen.

We're capable of creating a kind of soul double, an image we project to those we lead in order to maintain a calculated degree of distance and safety. We can even develop multiple versions for distinct settings. The image resembles us, but it's what author Brennan Manning called "the Imposter," or the

1. John 15:5.

A Word to Leaders and Pastors

"false self." He said of it, "Living out of the false self creates a compulsive desire to present a perfect image to the public so that everybody will admire us and nobody will know us."[c]

Veneers take on any number of forms. Allow me to mention a handful and see if any look familiar:

- **Strategic humor:** using quick wit, funny storytelling, sarcasm, and other displays of humor to keep a conversation shallow when it might otherwise be headed toward a request for deeper self-revelation; nothing disrupts a descent into uncomfortable truth like a well-timed joke

- **Selective disclosure:** referencing past experiences and present challenges in general and vague terms only; broad, nonspecific reflections create the illusion of disclosure without providing further opportunity for heart-level inquiry

- **Deflective others-focus:** redirecting introspective questions and personal application invitations toward those being shepherded and off the one doing the asking; what appears to be others-focused care serves to turn the spotlight away from the leader's own weaknesses and inadequacies

- **Definitive Bible citation:** quoting pertinent Scripture as the final word on a subject, circumventing further discussion that could involve probing personal issues; Bible scholarship can make for an excellent force field around heart vulnerability

- **Tactical misdirection:** deftly steering conversations away from topics that could expose uncomfortable history or unwanted scrutiny; the ability to change the

151

subject without detection keeps surprise parties secret
and unpleasant interactions evaded

- **Overt avoidance:** finding ways to simply not be found
  in environments where personal and private perspectives are pursued; a ministry filled with utilitarian
  relationships and productivity-focused programs conveniently limits opportunities to be asked the condition of one's soul

I wonder which of these veneers, or others, you might
recognize in yourself. If we identify and eliminate the veneers
masking our true condition, we can open the path to leading
from a healthy, honest soul.

Lead by Example

As we build soul-open authenticity into our own lives, it will
overflow naturally into our ministry to others. We're now
in a position to establish an ethos for our entire ministry
circle, to shape an environment where heart-level honesty
and soul-to-soul relationships are valued, encouraged, and
honored.

Consider some very tangible steps that can help you lead
by example in that direction.

- **Explicitly, publicly, and frequently state your intention** to make your ministry sphere an environment
  where people can bring and present their truest
  selves without fear. In small groups, studies, teaching or preaching settings, worship services, and
  everywhere—reiterate it as a bedrock value and invite
  it as an expected practice.

- **Take the lead in displaying Level 3 honesty yourself,** even if others aren't yet ready to do so. It's often said that you can't give away what you don't have. Employ the discretion and wisdom mentioned in the chapter on boundaries, then consistently model a transparent heart in your ministry settings. Allow others to see the true you, then patiently invite them to reveal the true them.

- **Practice pursuing others' hearts from a spirit of grace and acceptance.** Ask the kinds of questions that encourage those you lead to look below the surface of their own situations,[d] and show them you will value and protect their honest responses. Genuinely grant them permission to do the same with you.

- **Make applications from God's Word to your own life in the present tense,** not just the past tense. Push through the natural aversion to exposing active, unresolved issues, and talk about how current situations are affecting your thinking, emotions, and spiritual state in the here and now.

- **Model an open soul** in your leadership, your teaching, your marriage and family, and your friendships and fraternities. And if by chance you've acquired a "preacher's voice," or a distinct public prayer lingo, for heaven's sake, lose it. Speak, teach, and pray from your natural, authentic self.

- **Find or form a band of brothers or a circle of sisters** who share your commitment to unguarded camaraderie and let them know you want to count on them, be on their watch, and see them as the safe haven your soul needs.

Leading from an open soul produces a refreshing breed of spiritual shepherds. They become winsome and approachable, exhibiting a genuineness that draws those around them to the same intimacy with God and others they've come to enjoy. They find themselves able to fully empathize, not merely sympathize. They can climb into the trenches of others' pain and dirt without caring how soiled they might look . . . because their own muddy condition is already on display.

And their vulnerability and honesty prove contagious. Others embrace the gospel-drenched security these leaders revel in, liberating them from fear and shame and moving them closer to both God and each other in the acceptance they've found.

Perhaps just as importantly, they become healthier and more deeply connected themselves. They form heart-level friendships, find support and encouragement, and are lifted up even while they're lifting others.

The family of God desperately needs this kind of leader. May it be the kind we all aspire to be.

Discussion/Reflection Questions for Group or Individual Use

Chapter 1

Three Levels of Honesty

1. Read Proverbs 20:5.
   - How would you rephrase this verse in your own words?
   - Why do you think God says our inmost self needs to be drawn out?
   - How do you think someone could go about doing that?
2. Chapter 1 includes this statement:

   There's a "you" that you present to your world.
   - What words describe the "you" that you typically present?

- Which of those words is most accurate of the true you? Which is the least?
- Why do you think you present that version of yourself?

3. Look at the sample Scriptures the chapter listed that reference interactions specifically emitting from the heart:

> *Speak the truth from the heart (Ps. 15:2)*
> *Draw near to God with your heart (Heb. 10:22)*
> *Love each other deeply from the heart (1 Pet. 1:22)*
> *Forgive your brother or sister from your heart (Matt. 18:35)*
> *Sing and make music in your heart to the Lord (Eph. 5:19)*
> *Love the Lord with all your heart (Deut. 6:5)*
> *Serve from your heart (Deut. 10:12)*
> *Praise the Lord with your heart (Pss. 9:1; 86:12; 111:1; 138:1)*
> *Do the will of God from your heart (Eph. 6:6)*
> *Open wide your hearts (2 Cor. 6:13)*

- Why do you think the Bible adds phrases like "from the heart" and "in your heart" so often when it could have simply made the statement without them?
- Pick one of the scriptural activities listed above. How would you describe the difference between doing that "from the heart" and doing it from Level 1 or Level 2?
- What percentage of your actions in that particular area would you say currently engage your truest heart?

156

4. Three degrees of relationship, honesty, and self-disclosure were distinguished in the reading:

     Level 1 (Externals)
     Level 2 (Internals)
     Level 3 (Heart)

   • What would be an example of a Level 1 interaction/relationship with others in your life? A Level 2 interaction/relationship? A Level 3 interaction/relationship?

   • Why do you think it is so difficult and so rare for people to engage others with Level 3 self-exposure and honesty?

5. This question was asked about Level 3 honesty and relationship:

   Is there a place where this level of interaction happens in your current relationships? Who do you allow to see this deeply within you?

   • How would you answer?

   • What contributes to making your answer what it is?

6. How many people have you consistently seen live at heart-level self-disclosure and honesty with others?

   • What do you notice about them and their relationships?

   • What most holds you back from living that way yourself?

7. How motivated are you right now to pursue the kind of Level 3 honesty described in chapter 1?

   • What would need to happen to see that motivation level increase?

Chapter 2

Why We Keep Our Hearts Hidden

1. The chapter listed these negative outcomes we may have experienced that could make us reluctant to expose our truest selves:

   Rejection and condemnation
   Betrayal and abuse
   Repercussion and loss
   Disappointment and unhelpful response
   Unwanted obligation
   Little perceived value

   • Which do you think is most common?

   • Which have you experienced firsthand? How did it affect you?

2. The reading described how the sinful condition of our hearts makes us susceptible to shame and fear, subsequently driving us to hide our true selves.

   • Why would you say that fear is so intense?

   • How have you seen shame and/or fear personally affect you and your relationships?

3. Six negative effects of living with a closed-off heart were mentioned:

   It isolates us.
   It drains us.
   It hardens us.
   It weakens our self-awareness.
   It pressurizes our issues.
   It deadens us.

   • Which of these do you think is most common in people? Why?

- How have you seen one affect someone you know?

- Which one has been most true in your own life?

4. Read the Genesis 3 account of Adam hiding from exposure of his flawed condition and God's call for Adam to show himself. The chapter made this statement about that episode:

   The coverings God fashioned for Adam and his wife in the garden weren't given to hide their true condition. They were provided to cover their shame.

   - Do you agree or disagree? Why?

   - What is the difference between those two purposes/motivations (hiding true condition vs. covering shame)?

5. Read John 3:20–21 in light of the Genesis 3 exchange between God and Adam.

   - How would you say you have responded to God's call to come out of hiding about your heart's true condition?

   - What do you think will happen if you choose to show your true self more openly?

6. The chapter pointed to the gospel—the cleansing of Christ given freely through his death and resurrection to those who embrace it by faith—as the key that frees our hearts from shame and guilt.

   - How do you think the gospel accomplishes that?

   - How aware are you that you have personally received that cleansing through an act of faith?

7. Reflect on this excerpt from the chapter about our hearts' need for ongoing contact with the gospel:

   This conscious connection of your broken spirit to its restorer isn't just the one-time act of regeneration. It's also the delivery system for ongoing doses of the gospel's reanimating effect on your soul. It's not just the way to salvation; it is the way of salvation. We consistently need the gospel. To refresh our exposure to it. To consistently bring our exposed hearts back to its rejuvenating vitality. To submerge our souls in its restorative waters. Every. Single. Day.

   • In practical terms, what are some ways someone can engage their heart with the gospel daily?

   • How regularly would you say you do so in your current routine?

Chapter 3

Anatomy of an Open Soul

1. Read Genesis 1:26–27 and 2:7, which record how God gave humankind the unique possession of a *nephesh* (soul) capable of imaging unique aspects of God's personhood back to himself and to the world.

   • How generally aware are you of your soul's presence, activity, and condition? What increases or decreases that awareness?

   • How would you describe the condition of your soul at this moment? What would you say has most influenced that condition?

2. Reflect on the various components of personhood through which your soul interacts with its world:

Intellect (Mind)

Emotions (Spirit)

Activity (Body)

- How would you describe the difference between these important components of personhood and the soul itself?

- Which do you think tends to get the most attention when people think about gauging their spiritual health and maturity?

3. The chapter discussed the common, outside-in approach to producing change in the human heart, which tends to focus primarily on one or more of our intellect, emotions, and behaviors.

- What's an example of practices or programs you've seen that focus on the pursuit of spiritual health and maturity through an outside-in approach?

- What limitations or risks do you see in that approach?

4. Read through the passages used to illustrate how God doesn't equate external habits with heart-level transformation:

Jeremiah 6:20

Ezekiel 33:31

Colossians 2:23

Matthew 23:25, 27–28

- How would you describe the difference between entering into spiritual activities with and without your soul/heart first being engaged?

- In what ways might you be prone to equate external habits with heart transformation in your own approach to spiritual health?

5. Interact with this statement from the reading:

   Chances are, some of the most un-Christlike people you've met are also among the most biblically knowledgeable. Some of the harshest, most graceless, judgmental individuals in your life may also be those who seldom miss a Sunday service or church program. Some of the people exposed as hiding the darkest sin habits are also those you've watched pray most eloquently, tithe most generously, serve most faithfully, and lead most dynamically.

   - Without naming names, talk about an example where you have witnessed this kind of duplicity firsthand.

   - In what ways have you seen similar duplicity in yourself?

6. The reading used the analogy of "engaging the core" as part of an inside-out alternative to spiritual health and growth. Look again at the passages referenced for doing that:

   Deuteronomy 10:16
   Joel 2:13
   Jeremiah 29:13
   Psalm 139:23
   Matthew 23:26
   Psalm 51:17

   - What is a tangible way a person could enact the distinction and instructions given in those passages and engage their core first?

7. The chapter concluded with an exercise for making direct soul contact with Christ.

   • Did you actively engage in the exercise? If not, what kept you from doing so? If so, did you find it easy or difficult? Why?

   • What can you learn from the exercise that can apply to your awareness of your soul's presence and your willingness to acknowledge its current condition?

Chapter 4

Getting Honest with Yourself

1. The chapter described four of the most common ways we tend to lie to ourselves:

   Self-delusion: believing something about ourselves that simply isn't true

   Self-deception: not believing something about ourselves that is true

   Self-denial: telling ourselves we aren't carrying negative effects of mistreatment or perceived wrongdoing

   Self-diversion: avoiding honest introspection altogether

   • Which of the four do you think is most common?

   • Pick one of the four and give an example of how you've observed it in someone.

   • Which would you say you're most prone toward? Why do you think that is?

2. The reading stated that if we acknowledge the truth about our own condition and limitations, then

163

embrace the forgiveness and worth given in God's grace, we can experience a freedom that allows us to make three liberating declarations:

> *I'm not special, and I don't need to be.*
> *I'm not innocent, and I don't need to pretend I am.*
> *I'm not unscarred, and I don't need to convince myself that I am.*

- Which do you find most difficult to admit? Why?
- Pick one of the declarations and apply it to a current attitude or situation in your life. How would embracing it affect your thinking or actions?

3. The chapter challenged what it called "a misguided notion"—that *"to acknowledge the influence, or even the presence, of pain and injury in our souls is to admit a lack of trust in the God who always prevails, who works all things together for the good of those who love him."*

- Do you agree or disagree with the critique? Why?
- What has been your own experience with attempting to live "above" the effects of pain, defeat, and discouragement?
- In what ways have you seen that mentality pressure you away from admitting how you genuinely feel?

4. When was the last time you asked yourself what you were really feeling?

- How difficult was it to answer honestly?
- How easily would you say you give yourself permission to admit you're angry? Wounded? Frustrated? Discontent?

164

5. The reading called on heart-honest people to "experience soul weakness" and to be willing to "sit in its heartache."

   • When you're in the throes of a situation you genuinely anguish over, how readily do you acknowledge and embrace what you're feeling?

   • Do you feel pressure to deny those emotions or muster up a positive perspective to drown out the truth?

6. Choose one or two of the passages that referenced David's and Paul's self-descriptions about their situations and their effects and reread them:

   Psalm 13
   Psalm 25:16–22
   Psalm 31:9–18
   2 Corinthians 1:8–11
   2 Corinthians 12:7–10

   • What strikes you most about the honesty conveyed in the selected passage?

   • What lessons do you think you can learn from these autobiographical statements?

7. The chapter made this statement:

   Pretense is the enemy of an open soul. God doesn't want us to deny who we are or what we feel; he wants us to be active participators in our frailty.

   • Where do you currently feel the most pressure to display pretense?

   • What would a step toward unpretentious honesty look like in that setting?

   • How ready are you to pay the price that full authenticity might cost you there?

Chapter 5

What It Takes to Live Open-Hearted with Others

1. The chapter identified three "activators" of open-hearted living toward others:

   Full disclosure—revealing the current, truest condition of how we're doing and what is affecting us

   True confessions—exposing the sins we've committed, both present and past

   Teachable spirit—inviting input, guidance, and correction from others

   - How readily would you say you've enacted these practices in the past?
   - Which is most difficult for you to enact? Why?

2. Reflect on and answer these two questions asked in the reading:

   ○ *When was the last time you raised a loud, spontaneous cheer with someone over their good news or personal accomplishment?*

   ○ *When was the last time you shed actual, physical tears with another over something one of you was enduring?*

   - How often do each of those happen in your life?
   - What effect does it have on you when they do?
   - What does the regularity, or lack of regularity, of each tell you?

3. The chapter made this statement:

   No one should ever die with a secret.

   - Do you agree or disagree?

166

- Why would it be important for others to know something about us that they weren't necessarily involved in or affected by?

4. Interact with this statement from the reading:

    Soul-level connectivity, where we expose the dark recesses of our condition to each other, allows God's Spirit residing within us to deliver his strength, wisdom, and continued cleansing directly into one another's hearts.

    - How can strength, wisdom, and cleansing be dispensed from one person to another?
    - Have you ever seen it done? If so, describe it.

5. Read James 5:13–19, where believers are called on to openly confess their sins to others.

    - On a scale of 1 (lowest) to 10 (highest), how ready and willing do you feel right now to enact that instruction?
    - What could increase that number?
    - What else do you notice from that passage that is related to or affected by open-hearted confession?

6. With whom would you say you currently have the kind of bond the chapter describes?

    - Who *could* you have that kind of bond with if you pursued it?

7. Reflect on this question from the chapter:

    What secrets—the ones you've decided are best taken to your grave—are you still carrying?

    - What scares you most about opening this part of your life to another person?
    - How would you answer the question?

Chapter 6

God's Ingenious Design for Authentic Community

1. The chapter led with descriptions of two different Christian groups—one experiencing authentic, soul-open connection and another (Sarah's group) lacking it.

   • Which has been closer to your own experiences in groups? What made it so?

   • How has your involvement in either type of group affected you?

2. Three specific components critical to the formation of genuine, soul-open koinonia were given in the reading:

   The vertical "pipeline" of heart-to-heart connection with Christ's love

   The horizontal "pipelines" of heart-to-heart connection among Christ-indwelt people

   The active "one anothers" dispensing Christ's grace and truth to each other

   • Which do you think is most lacking in Christian "fellowship" groups today?

   • Which one do you personally find the toughest to enact? Why?

   • How can someone practically enact each?

   • If you have seen these components put into practice among a group of believers in the past, what did you observe about that group?

3. The chapter stated that God's agape love is manifested tangibly (first by Jesus, now by his followers) through two complementary elements: grace and truth.

- When it comes to displaying these elements toward others, which comes more easily to you?
- Have the groups and Christian environments you have been part of leaned more toward one or the other? If so, in which direction? Why do you think that is so?
- Do you think grace and truth can be displayed simultaneously in real-time human interactions? How?

4. The reading described Jesus's "new command" as being *new* because it called on believers to exhibit a "dual-pipeline" connection, dispensing love with one another.
   - How easily do you open the first pipeline to dispense agape love to others?
   - How easily do you open the second pipeline to receive doses of agape love from others?
   - What most prevents you from having both pipelines fully open?

5. Where (if anywhere) have you seen the kind of koinonia described in the chapter?
   - How often, and to what degree, would you say koinonia happens in your current group environment?
   - What would most need to happen to move your current group more toward the biblical description of fully functioning koinonia?

6. Read through Romans 12:9–21 (if possible, read the paraphrase found in the chapter aloud), then select one or more of the questions posed in the chapter about the actions it describes:

169

- When was the last time you were in an environment where you actually, literally, observed this particular act happening?
- Can this statement be accurately made about your group?
- What gets in the way of this practice occurring in your own circle of relationships?
- What would happen if you initiated this act in your current group or friendship circle?
- Do you currently have an environment where this aspect of spiritual community doesn't yet happen but could be introduced?

7. On a scale of 1 (lowest) to 10 (highest), how genuinely interested or motivated would you say you currently are to be part of a group that lives out the "heart-level community" described in the chapter? Why?

Chapter 7

How to Make Soul-Connected Community Happen

1. The chapter discussed the importance of "intentionality"—consistently and overtly restating the purpose of pursuing open-hearted community— for a group of Christ followers to experience koinonia.
- What difference do you think it could make for a group to have that purpose regularly articulated?
- How would you communicate that purpose if you were leading a group desiring to experience koinonia?

2. Reflect on this statement from the reading:

   When it comes to creating an environment where people push through their self-protective barriers and expose their true heart's condition to each other, someone has to be the first to jump in the pool.

   • Talk about a specific time when you, or someone in a group you were part of, took the risk of revealing something about their true heart's condition. How did people respond?

   • Why do you think this component is so important?

3. Think about the significance of what the chapter called "mutuality"—active participation in heart-open interaction and ministry among *everyone*—in a Christian community environment.

   • In your experience, has ministry movement within your groups been done by everyone in the group equally, by a handful of people, or by just one or two? Why do you think that has been the pattern?

   • What is the potential risk of inviting everyone in a group to act on their impulse to minister to another during a group gathering? What is the potential benefit? Do you think it's worth the risk? Why or why not?

4. Read Hebrews 10:24–25 and consider its implications for how consistently group participants gather and connect in the rhythms of everyday life.

   • What would you say to members of a group whose only contact with each other tends to happen during group meetings?

171

- Why do you think people in our current culture tend to be so hit-or-miss in their commitment to groups formed around koinonia? What could change that?

5. The chapter mentions the Protestant Reformation tenet of "the priesthood of all believers." Read one or more of these passages that speak to aspects of that principle:

    1 Corinthians 12:4–31
    Ephesians 4:4–16
    1 Timothy 2:5
    Hebrews 4:14–16
    1 Peter 2:4–9

    - What strikes you about the privileges and responsibilities all believers are given as credentialed "priests" to approach and serve God directly?

    - What are the implications of this principle for how a group functions in open-hearted community with each other?

6. The reading gave an example of a leader named Tyler who challenged his group to make it a true koinonia environment.

    - Read his statement again and reflect on what would happen if you or someone in your current group were to issue a similar challenge.

    - How would *you* respond if someone in your current group issued such a challenge?

7. What would it look like for you to "jump in the pool with your tux on" with a group of others?

Chapter 8

Soft Heart, Firm Boundaries

1. The chapter led off with this axiom of life:

   Any truly good idea will eventually be monetized, weaponized, or both.

   • What are some examples?

   • What is it about human nature that makes that statement true?

2. Four biblical guidelines were given that should inform our installation of wise boundaries for divulging our innermost thoughts and experiences:

   The principles of discretion and propriety
   The principle of discernment
   The law of love
   The exercise of faith

   • Which do you think is most often forgotten or neglected?

   • Can you think of an example of a time when you didn't enact one and saw negative consequences as a result?

   • Which do you personally find easiest to enact? Which do you find most difficult? Why?

3. The chapter mentioned two types of people with whom boundaries should be established:

   The "weak"
   The "fool"

   • How would you characterize each?

   • How would you recognize someone who is showing evidence of being "weak"? What would a healthy boundary with them look like?

173

- How would you identify someone who exhibits the qualities of a "fool"? What would a healthy boundary with them look like?

4. Read Proverbs 26:4–5.

- Give an example of a time you think verse 4 would be the wisest way to respond to a fool.

- Give an example of a time you think verse 5 would be the wisest way to respond to a fool.

5. Read the account of Jesus sending the disciples out to represent him in Matthew 10:5–31.

- What do you learn about being both soft-hearted and open-souled, and yet "wise as serpents" (KJV) in dealing with those who misuse or abuse vulnerabilities?

- How do you think a person can practically live out a vulnerable, honest, open heart toward others while still implementing the wisdom to guard against abuse?

6. How would you describe the difference between someone who lives from a fully authentic, open heart as God describes it and someone who is "brutally honest"?

7. Pick one of these passages referenced in the chapter and summarize how it applies to the practice of operating with a soft, open heart with firm, wise boundaries:

    Proverbs 15:1
    Ephesians 4:15
    Galatians 6:1
    Ephesians 4:25–26
    Romans 12:17–18

Chapter 9

What Happens When You Get Soul-Honest with Jesus

1. The chapter looked at the "vine and branches" connection: bringing a consciously opened heart into direct contact with Christ's heart.

   • How would you describe the difference between being generally aware of Jesus and being actively connected with him?

2. Reread the "abide in me" directive Jesus gave his disciples in John 15:4–10.

   • "Abide in me" means to stay in conscious, spirit-to-spirit connection with Christ's heart of love. How often would you say that is part of your current practice?

   • How do you know if you are abiding in a given moment?

   • What most affects your practice of abiding, either negatively or positively?

3. The chapter listed three suggested practices to move toward abiding in Christ:

   Intentional focus
   Passive positioning
   Active absorption

   • How would you summarize what each means in your own words?

   • Which one comes most naturally to you?

   • Which requires the most effort from you?

   • Describe an experience where you felt like you successfully implemented one or more of these suggested practices.

4. Talk about a time you felt like Jacob in Genesis 32:23–32, when you actively "wrestled" with God.

   • What was the wrestling most focused on?

   • What resulted from the wrestling?

5. On a scale of 1 (lowest) to 10 (highest), how would you assess your current regularity and meaningful awareness of "practicing the presence of God"? Why?

6. The reading sampled several "Level 3 honest" interactions David had with God.

   • What is your biggest personal block to expressing your truest feelings and perspectives that honestly with him?

7. The chapter emphasized the difference between *knowing God* and *knowing about God*.

   • How would you summarize the difference?

   • What practical advice would you give someone to ensure they are opening their truest selves to God in a way that results in them actually knowing him better?

Chapter 10

Facilitating Heart-Open Koinonia

1. The chapter emphasized the importance of establishing "*a clear picture of koinonia as the purpose and goal*" for a group seeking heart-level, soul-honest community.

   • Reread Acts 2:42–47 or Romans 12:4–21, and put into your own words a statement you would make to a group to communicate the vision of biblical koinonia.

- In what current environment could you make such a statement? How do you think those present would respond?

2. Reflect on this suggestion in the reading:

   Provide an opportunity at the start of the gathering for everyone to personally and individually approach God heart-to-heart and to engage intimately with their Creator.

   - How would you phrase such an invitation if you were leading a group through that exercise?
   - When was the last time you consciously accepted that invitation for yourself?

3. The chapter included a set of samples and questions that can "*invite the [group] participants to reveal their hearts and lives to each other.*"

   - Which one or two of the samples would you consider the best to use?
   - How adept would you say you currently are at "pursuing" people by asking further questions? Who is someone in your life right now that you think could benefit from you doing so?

4. Think about how enacting Scripture's "one anothers" in a group setting can help create an environment where heart-level, soul-honest community can flourish.

   - Which of the Bible's "one anothers" or spiritual gifts do you most commonly see put into action in the context of believer's groups you are part of? Which do you see least?
   - What was the last "one another" or spiritual gift you personally enacted *during* a gathering? What

most holds you back from doing so more often?
What could you do to change that?

5. The chapter urged steering a small group's formal Scripture study components toward heart-open, Level 3 honest interaction and application.

- How would you summarize the difference between Level 1 (content-focused), Level 2 (principle-focused), and Level 3 (application-focused) Bible study in a group setting? Which level do the groups you're typically part of tend toward?

- Think about the most recent passage of Scripture you've personally studied. Now look again at the three questions the chapter lists for interacting with the Bible at Level 3 and answer each for yourself:

  ○ *In what situation or relationship does the truth or instruction conveyed in this passage show up in your life today?*

  ○ *To what degree would you say you're implementing, or not implementing, this principle or practice in your current situations and choices? If you're not, what is holding you back?*

  ○ *What do you need to do about it? How are you going to think, feel, choose, or act differently to reflect this truth in your current situation?*

6. Look again at the list of ten "koinonia killers" referenced in the reading.

- Which do you think is most common? Which have you observed to be most distracting or destructive?

- Which are you most prone toward yourself?

7. The chapter made this statement:

   Biblical community extends to the routines of life, where the participants' relational circles expand to involve each other in daily practices. Serving one another, caring for each other, carrying one another's burdens—all require consistent touch points beyond a standing meeting.

   • Make a list of five natural, intentional ways people living in koinonia could involve others in their group in their everyday lives. Choose one you can initiate this week.

   • What most keeps you from involving others in your daily practices? What needs to change to make that more a part of your lifestyle?

Acknowledgments

I've never had an original idea in my life.

And that statement only further reinforces the point . . . because I didn't come up with it either. It was probably Mark Twain or Charles Spurgeon or C. S. Lewis—they always seem to get credited when we don't actually know who first said something.

This book is similarly the product of countless others' thoughts, influences, and refinements. I'd like to believe— and I certainly hope it's true—that the foundational principles come directly from God through his Word. But the framing of their understanding and their application to contemporary practice reflect the contributions of a tremendous collection of people without whom the end product would never have come to be.

My studies under Larry Crabb and Dan Allender deeply impacted my understanding of the human heart, authentic spiritual community, and the place of the church as God's instrument for personal transformation.

My longtime ministry supervisor, mentor, and friend Kevin Huggins didn't just teach open-hearted living, he consistently and relentlessly lived it, invited me to develop it, and guided me to cultivate it in others.

Over the years I was blessed to spend invaluable time with Dallas Willard and Brennan Manning, each of whom—in his own way—profoundly shaped my awareness of God's desire for heart-to-heart connection both with himself and among his people.

The body of Christ at Life Community Church of Hilliard, Ohio, served as a proving ground for a local church's capacity to embrace these principles as a core value and show they could be consistently lived out on a church-wide scale. It was my absolute joy to be called their pastor for more than twenty years, and they can't begin to know how far and wide their example and impact continue to reach.

Rocky Rocholl, president of the Fellowship of Evangelical Churches, with which I proudly serve, leads from the most humble heart I've ever seen in a denominational head and has made soul-level authenticity and community a driving passion behind how leaders are shaped and equipped, churches are planted and shepherded, and the gospel is proclaimed. His example continues to inspire me.

Brian Vos, Robin Turici, and the team at Baker Books have been tremendous partners in this endeavor. They didn't just believe in the message of this book enough to bring it to publication but they have also painstakingly worked to make it the best version of itself it could be. I'm grateful for their collaboration.

My personal peer review team sacrificed significant time and energy—and may have occasionally felt like they were testing our friendship—to offer excruciatingly honest critique, feedback, and suggestions on the manuscript. If the final product is in any way deemed worth reading, Nate Hamblin, Steve Adriansen, Phil Shomo, Tim Tabor, Tom Zimmerman, and Marcia Bennardo are the ones to thank.

And about the last name on that list—not only is my wife Marcia an exceptionally good editor in her own right (Baker should seriously hire her) but she's someone who lives out the message of this book every day of her life. Nearly forty years of marriage have proven, over and again, what everybody knew from the moment we first got together—I married way, way up. My heart still leaps every time she walks in the room.

Above all else, the One who deserves the greatest thanks is also the One I most desire to live an open-hearted life with: my Savior and Lord, Jesus Christ. He didn't just die and rise to reclaim my deadened soul, he continues to patiently show me how to live from a restored one. While I deeply hope and pray this work can be a transforming tool in others' lives, what I desire infinitely more is to know and walk with my Savior from a fully open, fully honest heart myself—praising and thanking him forever as the One who brought mine to life.

Notes

Introduction

a. Curt Thompson, *The Soul of Shame: Retelling the Stories We Believe about Ourselves* (Downers Grove, IL: InterVarsity, 2015), 138.

b. The Greek word *zōē* (ζωή), flourishing life, in contrast to *bios* (βίος), biological life. Used 135 times in the New Testament, including most references to "eternal life" (e.g., Matthew 7:14; John 1:4; 3:15–16, 36; 4:14, 36; 5:24).

Chapter 1 Three Levels of Honesty

a. Count me among those living out the adage "The older I get, the better I was."

b. We'll do a deeper dive on the actual, biblical meaning of the word *fellowship* in chapter 6.

c. Genesis 2:7. The Hebrew word *nephesh* (שֶׁפֶן), translated here as "living soul," is the deepest, centermost part, the nucleus of personhood. A second Hebrew word, *lebab* (בְּבַל), most often translated "heart," is used to describe the soul when it is engaging with its Maker or its world. *Nephesh* and *lebab* are often used interchangeably. Chapter 3 further teases out this and other aspects of what makes up full "personhood."

Chapter 2 Why We Keep Our Hearts Hidden

a. Results of American Perspectives Survey, May 2021, conducted by the Survey Center of American Life. Reported in Daniel A. Cox, "The State of American Friendship: Change, Challenges, and Loss," Survey Center on American Life, June 8, 2021, https://www.americansurveycenter.org /research/the-state-of-american-friendship-change-challenges-and-loss/.

b. A recent survey puts the percentage of Americans who say they feel substantial degrees of personal loneliness at 61 percent. "Loneliness and the Workplace," Cigna Health and Life Insurance Company, 2020, www .cigna.com/static/www-cigna-com/docs/about-us/newsroom/studies -and-reports/combatting-loneliness/cigna-2020-loneliness-infographic .pdf.

c. Further explored in chapter 3.

Chapter 3 Anatomy of an Open Soul

a. The aforementioned *nephesh* in chapter 1 (see Genesis 2:7).

b. Or "image" (Genesis 1:26–27).

c. Scholars have debated these components of personhood for centuries, arguing over phrases like *bipartite* and *tripartite*, as if the goal is to "solve" how many distinct parts comprise a human or to reverse engineer how they're constructed. But the wonder of personhood cannot be dissected like a fetal pig in a science class. The point of Scripture's varying combinations is not to present an exhaustive list of assembled parts God used in forming humans but to indicate the whole of our being—everything that comprises the true, total self. I'll leave the theological wrangling over nuances to others and will, for our purposes, reference the most common terms and pertinent meanings.

d. Our purpose here is not to critique or devalue discipleship courses and programs. Many tremendously effective resources exist, and the spiritual disciplines invoked and prescribed in them can be key contributors to spiritual formation and growth. It is simply our intent to reset the order in which we understand true transformation occurs. First the heart, then the mind, emotions, and outward actions.

e. Lest this be considered a tasteless metaphor, remember that it's the book of Proverbs that invokes the picture of "a gold ring in a pig's snout" (11:22).

Chapter 4 Getting Honest with Yourself

a. Michael Ende, *The Neverending Story* (New York: Doubleday & Company, Inc., 1983), 86.

b. *The Neverending Story*, directed by Wolfgang Peterson (Warner Brothers, 1984).

c. Patrick R. Heck, Daniel J. Simons, and Christopher F. Chabris, "65% of Americans Believe They Are Above Average in Intelligence," *Plos One*, July 3, 2018, www.journals.plos.org/plosone/article?id=10.1371 /journal.pone.0200103.

d. The percentage of high school athletes who go on to play professionally on any level runs right at 0.2%, but I still take my glove to the stadium just in case they find themselves down a player and need to call me from the stands to fill in for a couple innings.

e. Maria Scinto, "You Probably Don't Look Younger Than Your Age," *The List*, February 22, 2021, www.thelist.com/253923/you-probably-dont-look-younger-than-your-age; "My Turn: We're Old Enough to Know Better When It Comes to Youthful Flattery," *Newsday*, January 30, 2020, www.newsday.com/lifestyle/retirement/my-turn-don-t-be-fooled-by-youthful-flattery-f50221.

f. *Monty Python and the Holy Grail*, directed by Terry Gilliam and Terry Jones (Python Pictures, April 3, 1975).

g. C. S. Lewis, *Mere Christianity* (New York: Macmillan, 1952).

h. *Taken*, directed by Pierre Morel (Twentieth Century Fox, January 30, 2009).

i. Timothy Keller, *The Meaning of Marriage: Facing the Complexities of Commitment with the Wisdom of God* (New York: Penguin Group, 2011).

j. Hannah Hurnard, *Hinds' Feet on High Places* (Sheffield, England: Christian Literature Crusade, 1955).

Chapter 5 What It Takes to Live Open-Hearted with Others

a. We'll look specifically into how we live open-hearted with God in chapter 9.

b. Matthew 26:38. Jesus used the word for *abide* in this exchange. In chapter 9 we'll see why that is significant in what he invited his friends to do.

c. Henry Cloud, *Changes That Heal* (Grand Rapids: Zondervan, 1990), 49.

d. Michael Slepian, "The Problem with Keeping a Secret," Society for Personality and Social Psychology, July 1, 2019, https://www.spsp.org/news-center/blog/slepian-keeping-secrets.

e. Some pushback to this idea exists in the Christian community, arguing the audience for confession should be limited to those directly victimized or affected by the sin (as described in passages like Colossians 3:13) or to a singular spiritual shepherd. To do otherwise, the argument goes, risks putting people in a position to judge or gossip. But the context, word choice, and grammar of James 5 make a clear distinction, describing an open confession made to those with whom we are functioning in spiritual community rather than only to victims. Scripture consistently uses the word *charizomai* (χαρίζομαι), "to seek pardon or forgiveness," for the act of approaching those we have directly sinned against, and *exomologeo* (ἐξομολογέω), meaning "to confess outwardly" (the word used in James 5:16), for the act of sin-admission in spiritual community among those not necessarily sinned against. I'll respectfully suggest that pushback against open confession may at times be motivated by either fear or a desire to create an out from uncomfortable vulnerability.

f. Ann Voskamp, *The Way of Abundance: A 60-Day Journey into a Deeply Meaningful Life* (Thomas Nelson, 2018), 94.

Chapter 6 God's Ingenious Design for Authentic Community

a. As described in numerous New Testament passages, such as Acts 2; Acts 4; 1 Corinthians 14; Ephesians 4; and Colossians 3.

b. I am grateful to Steve Adriansen, founder and director of Behind the Scenes Ministries, for this dual pipeline terminology and his insightful clarifications of what qualifies the "love one another" instruction of John 13–15 as a "new" command.

c. "The fellowship" is used in 2 Corinthians 13:14 to describe the connection "of the Holy Spirit" phrasing mirrored in Philippians 1:4–5. Paul uses it in Philemon 6 to refer to the interpersonal, shared influences Philemon could experience in his own journey when he writes, "I pray that *the fellowship* of your faith may become effective" (NASB, emphasis added).

Chapter 7 How to Make Soul-Connected Community Happen

a. A list of koinonia killers can be found in chapter 10.

b. Zamayirha Peter, "Pigcasso a Millionaire," City Press, January 10, 2019, https://www.news24.com/citypress/news/pigcasso-a-millionaire -20190110.

c. At the time, she didn't even realize she was living out a scriptural directive by doing so. See 1 Corinthians 14:26; Ephesians 5:19; Colossians 3:16.

Chapter 8 Soft Heart, Firm Boundaries

a. Henry Cloud and John Townsend's seminal work on biblical boundaries still stands as the vanguard on this crucial component of living from a free, opened, healthy soul. See BoundariesBooks.com.

Chapter 9 What Happens When You Get Soul-Honest with Jesus

a. Various translations render it "remain in," "dwell in," "dwell with," "stay united in," "be joined in," "live in," "continue in," and "stay connected to."

b. Edward W. Hellman, *Oregon Viticulture* (Corvallis: Oregon State University Press, 2003), 13.

c. My preference for most accurately conveying μείνατε ἐν ἐμοί ("abide in me") in English would be, "Stay in conscious, spirit-to-spirit connection with Christ's heart of love," but for purposes of brevity I will use the older English word *abide*.

d. The Hebrew word for "be still" is from *rapha* (רָפָה), which conveys a vivid picture of sinking slowly into something.

e. Brother Lawrence, *The Practice of the Presence of God with Spiritual Maxims* (Grand Rapids: Revell, 1958, 1967). Ebook edition created 2012.

f. Brother Lawrence, *The Practice of the Presence of God*.

g. Psalms 35:4–8; 58:6; 69:23; 109:9. These requests are almost certainly rooted in a desire for God's holy justice rather than fleshly vengeance. They are nonetheless passionate expressions of the heart's genuine state and reflections of personal experience.

Chapter 10 Facilitating Heart-Open Koinonia

a. Note that some participants who are reluctant to respond to this invitation may benefit from an offline, individual conversation outside the meeting time where they can be encouraged to open themselves up to the group when the opportunity is presented. Prayerful and patient discernment is important in guiding those new to the practice of self-exposure.

b. Two phrases should be forever banned from group fellowship and counseling settings. The first is "Thank you for sharing," which if not immediately followed with another question communicates that the listener feels awkward not knowing how to respond to what was just said and is grasping for filler and transition. It conveys disingenuous thanks and indicates the person should now consider their turn finished, with attention turning to someone else. The second is "Anyone else?" which also communicates, "The person who just spoke is finished; let's pivot to someone else," and shuts down the one who may have just revealed something that may need to be drawn out further.

c. See Luke 12:11–12. Though the context of this passage indicates times when adversaries challenge one's faith, the transferable principle is that the Spirit can fill willing vessels to speak God's message to others when they simply put themselves in a position to represent him.

Conclusion

a. *The Godfather*, directed by Francis Ford Coppola (Paramount Pictures, March 24, 1972).

Appendix

a. See 1 Samuel 8:5. Even Jesus was saddled with this expectation by his followers (John 6:14–15; Acts 1:6). He chose to lead from an open, honest, humble heart anyway.

b. Skye Jethani, *With: Reimagining the Way You Relate to God* (Nashville: Thomas Nelson, 2011).

c. Brennan Manning, *Abba's Child: The Cry of the Heart for Intimate Belonging* (Carol Stream, IL: Tyndale, 2015), 31.

d. Samples of these can be found in chapter 10.

Tom Bennardo is a four-decade veteran of ministry and spiritual formation. His experience spans the spectrum—church planter, lead pastor, mentor and coach, conference speaker, author, and denominational leader.

He holds an MDiv from Grace Theological Seminary and a doctorate from Trinity Evangelical Divinity School and currently serves as executive director of church leadership and multiplication for the Fellowship of Evangelical Churches, providing training, equipping, and spiritual direction for current and emerging pastors. He and his wife have two adult daughters and reside in San Clemente, California.

Connect with Tom:

TomBennardo.com

@TBennardo

@TomBennardo

@TomBennardo